PHILIP'S

BRITAIN & IRELAND

NIGEL HENBEST

STARGAZING 2023

MONTH-BY-MONTH GUIDE TO THE NIGHT SKY

www.philips-maps.co.uk

Published in Great Britain in 2022 by Philip's,
a division of Octopus Publishing Group Limited
(www.octopusbooks.co.uk)
Carmelite House, 50 Victoria Embankment,
London EC4Y ODZ
An Hachette UK Company (www.hachette.co.uk)

TEXT
Nigel Henbest © 2022 pp. 4–85, 90–95
Philip's © 2022 pp. 1–3
Robin Scagell © 2022 pp. 86–89

ARTWORKS © Philip's except pp. 13, 19, 25, 31, 37, 43, 49,
55, 61, 67, 73, 79 © Nigel Henbest/Philip's

ISBN 978-1-84907-617-3

Nigel Henbest has asserted his moral right under the
Copyright, Designs and Patents Act, 1988, to be identified
as the author of pp. 4–85 and 90–95 of this work.

A CIP catalogue record for this book is available from the
British Library.

Printed in China

Cover: Comet Leonard and M3.
Title page: Ring Nebula.

MIX
Paper from
responsible sources
FSC® C008047

Welcome to the latest edition of *Stargazing*! Within these pages, you'll find your complete guide to everything that's happening in the night sky throughout 2023 – whether you're a beginner or an experienced astronomer.

With the 12 monthly star charts, you can find your way around the sky on any night in the year. Impress your friends by identifying celestial sights ranging from the brightest planets to some pretty obscure constellations.

Every page of *Stargazing 2023* is bang up-to-date, bringing you everything that's new this year, from shooting stars to eclipses. And I'll start with a run-down of the most exciting sky sights on view in 2023 (opposite).

THE MONTHLY CHARTS

A reliable map is just as essential for exploring the heavens as it is for visiting a foreign country. So each monthly section starts with a circular **Star Chart** showing the whole evening sky.

To keep the maps uncluttered, I've plotted about 200 of the brighter stars (down to third magnitude), which means you can pick out the main star patterns – the constellations. (If the charts showed every star visible on a really dark night, there'd be around 3000 stars on each!) I also show the ecliptic: the apparent path of the Sun in the sky; it's closely followed by the Moon and planets as well.

You can use these charts throughout the UK and Ireland, along with most of Europe, North America and northern Asia – between 40 and 60 degrees north – though the detailed timings given apply specifically to the UK and Ireland.

USING THE STAR CHARTS

It's pretty easy to use the charts. Start by working out your compass points. South is where the Sun is highest in the sky during the day; east is roughly where the Sun rises, and west where it sets. At night, you can find north by locating the Pole Star – Polaris – by using the stars of the Plough (see March's Object).

The left-hand chart then shows your view to the north. Most of these stars are visible all year: the circumpolar constellations wheel around Polaris as the seasons progress. Your view to the south appears in the right-hand chart; it changes much more as the Earth orbits the Sun. Leo's prominent 'sickle' is high in the spring skies. Summer is dominated by the bright trio of Vega, Deneb and Altair. Autumn's familiar marker is the Square of Pegasus; while the stars of Orion rule the winter sky.

During the night, our perspective on the sky also alters as the Earth spins around, making the stars and planets appear to rise in the east and set in the west. The charts depict the sky in the late evening (the exact times are noted in the captions). As a rule of thumb, if you are observing two hours later, then the following month's map will be a better guide to the stars on view – though beware: the Moon and planets won't be in the right place.

THE PLANETS, MOON AND SPECIAL EVENTS

The charts also highlight the **planets** above the horizon in the late evening. I've

HIGHLIGHTS OF THE YEAR

- **1 January:** from central and northern regions of Britain and Ireland you'll see the Moon occult Uranus, starting at 10.15 pm.
- **Night of 3/4 January:** the maximum of the Quadrantid meteor shower is spoilt this year by bright moonlight.
- **22 January:** Saturn lies just 20 arcminutes above Venus.
- **15 February:** Venus passes only 20 arcminutes from Neptune: binoculars show the brightest and the dimmest planets at once (with Venus 60,000 times brighter than Neptune).
- **22 February:** the crescent Moon lies between the two most brilliant planets, Venus and Jupiter.
- **1 March:** the two brightest worlds, Venus and Jupiter, are just 35 arcminutes apart, low in the west after sunset.
- **20 April:** parts of Western Australia and Indonesia are treated to a hybrid solar eclipse, which changes from annular to total and back again. A partial eclipse is visible from all of Australia, Indonesia and the Philippines.
- **Night of 22/23 April:** it's an excellent year for observing the Lyrid meteor shower, as the Moon is well out of the way.
- **2 June:** Mars lies in the middle of the star cluster Praesepe.
- **9 July:** Venus reaches its greatest brilliance as an Evening Star.
- **Night of 12/13 August:** maximum of the Perseid meteor shower, putting on a spectacular display under dark skies.
- **27 August:** Saturn is opposite to the Sun in the sky, and closest to the Earth.
- **31 August:** the biggest and brightest supermoon of the year. Because it's the second Full Moon of the month, some people call it a 'blue supermoon'.

- **5 September:** the Pleiades lie just above the Moon, with Jupiter to the right and Aldebaran below.
- **18 September:** Venus reaches its greatest brilliance as a Morning Star.
- **19 September:** Neptune is opposite to the Sun, and at its nearest to the Earth.
- **14 October:** people in the western United States, central America, Colombia and Brazil are treated to an annular eclipse of the Sun: maximum eclipse, with 95 per cent of the Sun obscured, occurs over Nicaragua. A partial eclipse is visible from all the Americas.
- **Night of 21/22 October:** it's a great year for observing the Orionid meteor shower, debris from Halley's Comet smashing into Earth's atmosphere.
- **28 October:** there's a partial lunar eclipse, right next to Jupiter, though only 12 per cent of the Moon is obscured. Visible from Europe, Africa and Asia, the eclipse begins at 8.35pm and ends at 9.53 pm.
- **1 November:** Jupiter is closest to the Earth.
- **3 November:** Jupiter lies opposite to the Sun in the sky.
- **9 November, before dawn:** the crescent Moon pairs up with glorious Venus in the dawn sky. After sunrise, the Moon occults Venus (9.45–10.45 am).
- **13 November:** Uranus lies opposite to the Sun.
- **Night of 17/18 November:** the Leonid meteors reach their annual maximum.
- **Night of 2/3 December:** we may be treated to a rare display of the Andromedids, meteors from Biela's Comet, which disintegrated in 1846. You may see a shooting star every minute.
- **Night of 13/14 December:** the Geminids are the best annual meteor shower of the year, this year totally unspoilt by moonlight.

indicated the track of any **comets** known at the time of writing; though I can't guide you to a comet that's found after the book has been printed!

I've plotted the position of the Full Moon each month, and also the **Moon's position** at three-day intervals before and afterwards. If there's a **meteor** shower in the month, the charts show its radiant – the position from which the meteors stream.

The **Calendar** provides a daily guide to the Moon's phases and other celestial happenings. I've detailed the most interesting in the **Special Events** section, including close pairings of the planets, times of the equinoxes and solstices and – most exciting – **eclipses** of the Moon and Sun.

Check out the **Planet Watch** page for more about the other worlds of the Solar System, including their antics at times they're not on the main monthly charts. I've illustrated unusual planetary and lunar goings-on in the **Planet Event Charts**. There's a full explanation of planetary motions, eclipses and meteor showers in **Solar System 2023** on pages 80–82.

MONTHLY OBJECTS, TOPICS AND PICTURES

Each monthly section homes in on one particularly interesting **object**: a planet, a star or a galaxy. I also feature a spectacular **picture** – taken by an amateur based in Britain or Ireland – describing how the image was captured, and subsequently processed. And there's an in-depth exploration of a fascinating and often newsworthy **topic**, ranging from ancient Chinese astronomy to the multiverse.

GETTING IN DEEP

A practical **observing tip** is included each month, helping you to explore the sky with the naked eye, binoculars or a telescope.

Check out the guide to the **Top 20 Sky Sights**, such as nebulae, star clusters and galaxies. You'll find it on pages 83–85.

And equipment expert Robin Scagell checks out some state-of-the-art telescopes that are totally automatic: just set them down in your garden, and they'll find and image any celestial sight you request.

Finally, a brand-new section details the internationally approved dark-sky sites in Britain and Ireland, where you're guaranteed to be free of light pollution. It also includes a round-up of planetariums and public observatories you can visit, plus a guide to the best star parties and astronomical festivals.

Happy stargazing!

JARGON BUSTER

Have you ever wondered how astronomers describe the brightness of the stars or how far apart they appear in the sky? Not to mention how we can measure the distances to the stars? If so, you can quickly find yourself mired in some arcane astro-speak – magnitudes, arcminutes, light years and the like.

Here's our quick and easy guide to busting that jargon:

Magnitudes

It only takes a glance at the sky to see that some stars are pretty brilliant, while many more are dim. But how do we describe to other people how bright a star appears?

Around 2000 years ago, ancient Greek astronomers ranked the stars into six classes, or **magnitudes**, depending on their brightness. The most brilliant stars were first

magnitude, and the faintest stars you can see came in at sixth magnitude. So the stars of the Plough, for instance, are second magnitude while the individual Seven Sisters in the Pleiades are fourth magnitude.

Mars (magnitude –1.6 here) shines a hundred times brighter than the Seven Sisters in the Pleiades, which are around 5 magnitudes fainter.

Today, scientists can measure the light from the stars with amazing accuracy. (Mathematically speaking, a difference of five magnitudes represents a difference in brightness of one hundred times.) So the Pole Star is magnitude +2.0, while Rigel is magnitude +0.1. Because we've inherited the ancient ranking system, the brightest stars have the *smallest* magnitude. In fact, the most brilliant stars come in with a negative magnitude, including Sirius (magnitude –1.5).

And we can use the magnitude system to describe the brightness of other objects in the sky, such as stunning Venus, which can be almost as brilliant as magnitude –5. The Full Moon and the Sun have whopping negative magnitudes!

At the other end of the scale, stars, nebulae and galaxies with a magnitude fainter than +6.5 are too dim to be seen by the naked eye. Using ever larger telescopes – or by observing from above Earth's atmosphere – you can perceive fainter and fainter objects. The most distant galaxies visible to the Hubble Space Telescope are ten billion times fainter than the naked-eye limit.

Here's a guide to the magnitude of some interesting objects:

Sun	–26.7
Full Moon	–12.5
Venus (at its brightest)	–4.7
Sirius	–1.5
Betelgeuse (variable)	0.0 – +1.6
Polaris (Pole Star)	+2.0
Faintest star visible to the naked eye	+6.5
Faintest star visible to the Hubble Space Telescope	+31

Degrees of separation

Astronomers measure the distance between objects in the sky in **degrees** (symbol °): all around the horizon is 360°, while it's 90° from the horizon to the point directly overhead (the zenith).

As we show in the photograph, you can use your hand – held at arm's length – to give a rough idea of angular distances in the sky.

For objects that are very close together – like many double stars – we divide the degree into 60 arcminutes (symbol '). And for celestial objects that are extremely tiny – such as the discs of the planets – we split each arcminute into 60 arcseconds (symbol "). To give you an idea of how small these units are, it takes 3600 arcseconds to make up one degree.

Here are some typical separations and sizes in the sky:

Length of the Plough	25°
Width of Orion's Belt	3°
Diameter of the Moon	31'
Separation of Mizar and Alcor	12'
Diameter of Jupiter	45"
Separation of Albireo A and B	35"

How far's that star?

Everything we see in the heavens lies a long way off. We can give distances to the planets in millions of kilometres. But the stars are so distant that even the nearest, Proxima Centauri, lies some 40 million million kilometres away. To turn those distances into something more manageable, astronomers use a larger unit: one **light year** is the distance that light travels in a year.

One light year is about 9.46 million million kilometres. That makes Proxima Centauri a much more manageable 4.2 light years away from us. Here are the distances to some other familiar astronomical objects, in light years:

Sirius	8.6
Polaris	440
Centre of the Milky Way	26,700
Andromeda Galaxy	2.5 million
Most distant galaxies seen by the Hubble Space Telescope	13 billion

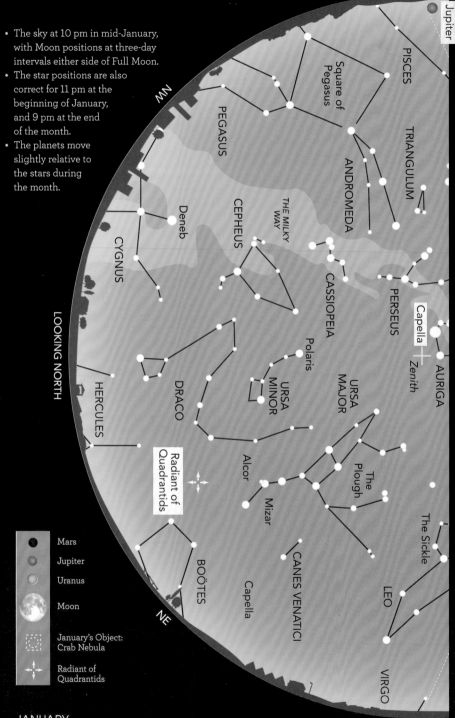

- The sky at 10 pm in mid-January, with Moon positions at three-day intervals either side of Full Moon.
- The star positions are also correct for 11 pm at the beginning of January, and 9 pm at the end of the month.
- The planets move slightly relative to the stars during the month.

WEST

Jupiter

PISCES

Square of Pegasus

TRIANGULUM

PEGASUS

ANDROMEDA

NW

Deneb

CEPHEUS

THE MILKY WAY

CASSIOPEIA

PERSEUS

Capella

Zenith

AURIGA

CYGNUS

LOOKING NORTH

Polaris

URSA MINOR

URSA MAJOR

HERCULES

DRACO

Alcor

The Plough

Radiant of Quadrantids

Mizar

CANES VENATICI

The Sickle

BOÖTES

Capella

LEO

NE

VIRGO

Mars

Jupiter

Uranus

Moon

January's Object: Crab Nebula

Radiant of Quadrantids

EAST

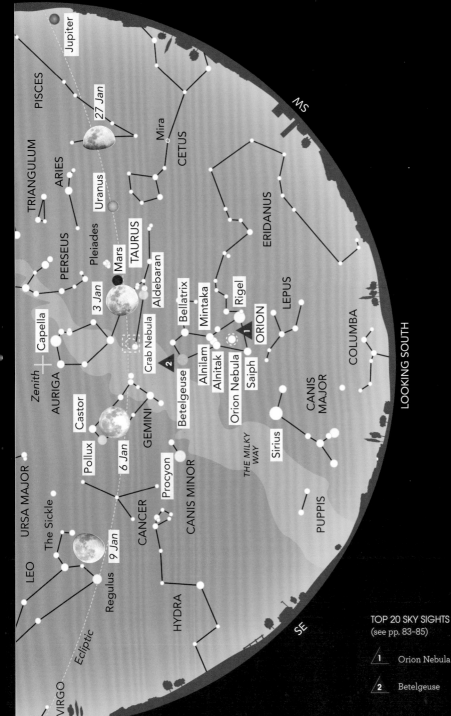

WEST

JANUARY

SW

LOOKING SOUTH

- Jupiter
- PISCES
- TRIANGULUM
- ARIES
- 27 Jan
- Mira
- CETUS
- PERSEUS
- Uranus
- Pleiades
- TAURUS
- Mars
- 3 Jan
- Aldebaran
- Crab Nebula
- Bellatrix
- Mintaka
- Rigel
- ERIDANUS
- LEPUS
- Capella
- Zenith
- AURIGA
- Alnilam
- Alnitak
- Orion Nebula
- Saiph
- ORION
- COLUMBA
- Castor
- Betelgeuse
- GEMINI
- CANIS MAJOR
- Pollux
- 6 Jan
- Procyon
- THE MILKY WAY
- Sirius
- URSA MAJOR
- The Sickle
- CANIS MINOR
- PUPPIS
- LEO
- 9 Jan
- CANCER
- Regulus
- HYDRA
- SE
- VIRGO
- Ecliptic
- EAST

TOP 20 SKY SIGHTS
(see pp. 83–85)

1 Orion Nebula

2 Betelgeuse

The evening sky puts on a spectacular show for the start of the year, with four brilliant planets on display – Venus, **Mars, Jupiter** and Saturn – plus a giant circlet of dazzling stars centred on magnificent **Orion: Sirius, Procyon, Pollux, Castor, Capella** and **Aldebaran.**

JANUARY'S CONSTELLATION

Striding across the sky is the familiar figure of **Orion**. According to Greek myth, this formidable hunter was the most handsome man on Earth. In the sky he also cuts a dash, with his seven major stars all placed in the 'Top 70' brightest stars in the sky.

Orion's Belt is marked by well-matched **Alnitak, Alnilam** and **Mintaka**, lying over 1200 light years away. Despite this immense distance, these stars appear brilliant to our view because each outshines our Sun 200,000 times over.

Look carefully below the Belt to spot a faint patch of light representing Orion's sword. This is the great **Orion Nebula**, a seething maelstrom of incandescent gas, 24 light years in diameter. It's the birthplace of new stars, created from a dark cloud of dust and gas.

Two hot stars outline the bottom of Orion's tunic: brilliant **Rigel** and its less showy sibling **Saiph**. His shoulders are picked out by **Bellatrix** and gaudy blood-red **Betelgeuse**, a giant star destined to blow itself apart as a supernova (see December's Object).

JANUARY'S OBJECT

Just above the lower 'horn' of **Taurus** (the Bull), Chinese astronomers witnessed a brilliant new 'guest star' in 1054. Visible in daylight for 23 days, it remained in the night sky for two years.

> ### OBSERVING TIP
>
> The brilliant winter constellations and planets are tempting us to spend plenty of time outside. So make sure you dress up warmly! Lots of layers are better than just a heavy coat, as they trap more air close to your skin. Heavy-soled boots with two pairs of socks stop the frost creeping up your legs. And a surprising amount of your body heat escapes through the top of your head, so complete your outfit with a beanie or – even better – a hat with ear flaps.

This supernova was the explosion of a star at the end of its life, and today we see its remains as the **Crab Nebula** – named by nineteenth-century astronomer the Third Earl of Rosse (1800-67) because he thought it resembled a crab's pincer. The expanding debris now measures 11 light years across. You can make out the Crab Nebula through a small telescope, but it is compact and faint (magnitude +8.4 and 6 arcminutes across).

At its centre, the core of the dead star has collapsed to become a superdense neutron star: an object with the mass of the Sun, but only the size of a city and spinning round 30 times a second.

JANUARY'S TOPIC: EXOPLANETS

When I started out in astronomy, the only planets known were the nine orbiting the Sun (then including Pluto).

Today, the total stands at over 5000 planets!

The new discoveries are exoplanets – worlds orbiting other stars in our Galaxy. Their colours range from blue to a deep magenta. Some planets are as white as snow, others as dark as coal. The youngest planet, Proplyd 133-353 in the Orion Nebula, is just half a million years old. Conversely, WASP-183b is almost as old as the Universe itself.

Many are 'hot Jupiters': large worlds – like Jupiter in our own Solar System – but baked to incandescence because they are orbiting so close to their sun. WASP-76b is so hot that its clouds are shedding raindrops made of molten iron!

At the opposite extreme are planets that have become detached from their sun: these 'rogue planets' freeze just a few degrees above the absolute zero of temperature.

The star TRAPPIST-1 has a collection of seven planets, all close to the Earth's size. At least one of these worlds probably has the right temperature and atmosphere for liquid water to exist on its surface. Here, 41 light years away in Aquarius, may reside our nearest cosmic neighbours.

JANUARY'S PICTURE

It's always a stunning sight when the two brightest objects in the night sky – the Moon and **Venus** – tango together, as they will on 23 January. Just over a year ago, the prospect enticed Bernie Brown to drive from his home in Belfast to the shores of Lough Neagh to enjoy a clear western horizon.

On 9 October 2021, Bernie Brown captured this image with a Canon R5 camera and Canon 70-200 mm f/2.8 IS II USM lens, set to 200 mm and ISO 400 with an exposure of 0.8 seconds.

Overcoming hazards that included threatening clouds, an irate swan and a missing bracket for his camera lens, Bernie succeeded in imaging this beautiful atmospheric view. And it didn't end there. People were out taking an evening stroll, and 'just seeing their excitement when I pointed out Venus, and explaining what was happening made it all the more special for me as they were going home with pictures of a special night by the water.'

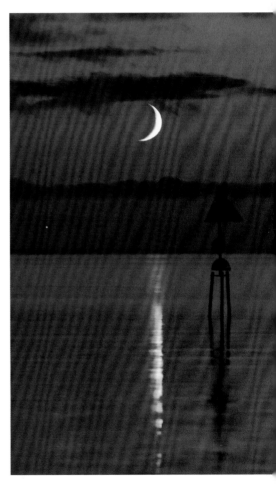

SUNDAY	MONDAY	TUESDAY	WEDNESDAY	THURSDAY	FRIDAY	SATURDAY
1 Moon occults Uranus	2 Moon near Pleiades	3 Moon very near Mars; Quadrantids	4 Quadrantids (am); Earth at perihelion	5	6 11.08 pm Full Moon near Castor and Pollux	7 Moon near Castor and Pollux
8 Moon near Praesepe	9 Moon near Regulus	10 Moon near Regulus	11	12	13	14 Moon near Spica
15 2.10 am Last Quarter Moon	16	17	18 Moon near Antares (am)	19	20	21 8.53 pm New Moon
22 Venus very near Saturn	23 Moon near Venus and Saturn	24	25 Moon near Jupiter	26	27	28 3.19 pm First Quarter Moon
29 Moon near Pleiades	30 Moon near Mars, Pleiades and Aldebaran; Mercury W elongation	31				

SPECIAL EVENTS

- **1 January:** if you're north of a line from Cork to Norwich, you'll see the Moon move in front of Uranus; south of that line, the seventh planet skims the lunar surface. Use binoculars or a small telescope to see the faint planet. Exact timings depend on your location, but watch from 10.15 pm onwards.

- **3 January:** the brilliant red 'star' right above the Moon is Mars (Chart 1a).

- **Night of 3/4 January:** maximum of the **Quadrantid meteor shower**, dust particles from the old comet 2003 EH₁ burning up in the Earth's atmosphere. It's one of most prolific meteor showers, but spoilt this year by bright moonlight.

- **4 January, 4.17 am:** the Earth is at perihelion, its closest point to the Sun (147 million km away).

- **22 January:** Venus lies only 20 arcminutes below Saturn. They are an unmatched pair, with the Evening Star some 75 times brighter than the ringworld.

- **23 January:** low in the south-west after sunset, the thinnest crescent Moon forms a stunning tableau with Venus and fainter Saturn (Chart 1b).

- **25 January:** Jupiter is above the crescent Moon.

- **30 January:** Mars lies above the Moon, with Aldebaran to the left and the Pleiades to the lower right.

1a 3 January, 10 pm. The Moon with Mars and the Pleiades.

1b 23 January, 6 pm. The crescent Moon near Venus and Saturn.

- Look to the south-west after sunset to spot brilliant **Venus**. At magnitude –3.9, the glorious Evening Star is brighter than any of the stars or other planets, and it will be gracing the dusk sky until July.

- Venus is moving up towards **Saturn**, which shines at magnitude +0.8 in Capricornus, and passes just below the ringworld on 22 January (see Special Events). The two planets set about 6.30 pm. They form a lovely grouping with the Moon on 23 January (Chart 1b).

- Higher up in the south we have two more brilliant planets. To the right is **Jupiter,** blazing at magnitude –2.3 in Pisces. The giant planet sets around 10.30 pm. The Moon is nearby on the evening of 25 January.

- **Mars** lies well to the left, among the stars of Taurus and near to Aldebaran and the Pleiades star cluster. It's rather fainter than Jupiter,

fading from magnitude –1.2 at the start of January to –0.3 by the end of the month. The Red Planet is setting about 5 am. The Moon glides right underneath Mars on 3 January (Chart 1a), and it's back in the vicinity of the Red Planet on 30 January.

- At magnitude +5.7, **Uranus** in Aries sets around 2.30 am. There's a convenient chance to find this faint planet on 1 January, when it's right next to the Moon: in fact, you

may be lucky enough to see Uranus disappear behind the Moon (see Special Events).

- **Neptune** (magnitude +7.9) lurks between Aquarius and Pisces, and sets about 9.30 pm.

- Look out for **Mercury** in the morning sky during the second half of January. The innermost planet is very low in the south-east before sunrise, and brightens from magnitude +0.4 to –0.1. It's at its greatest separation from the Sun on 30 January.

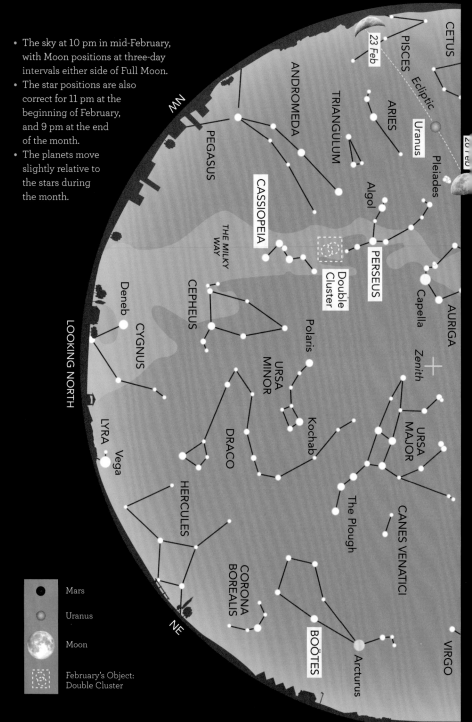

- The sky at 10 pm in mid-February, with Moon positions at three-day intervals either side of Full Moon.
- The star positions are also correct for 11 pm at the beginning of February, and 9 pm at the end of the month.
- The planets move slightly relative to the stars during the month.

WEST

CETUS

PISCES

Ecliptic

23 Feb

ARIES

Uranus

ANDROMEDA

TRIANGULUM

Pleiades

Algol

CASSIOPEIA

PEGASUS

THE MILKY WAY

PERSEUS

Double Cluster

Capella

AURIGA

NW

CEPHEUS

Deneb

Polaris

Zenith

Double

CYGNUS

URSA MINOR

Kochab

URSA MAJOR

LOOKING NORTH

DRACO

The Plough

CANES VENATICI

LYRA

Vega

HERCULES

CORONA BOREALIS

BOÖTES

Arcturus

VIRGO

NE

Mars

Uranus

Moon

February's Object:
Double Cluster

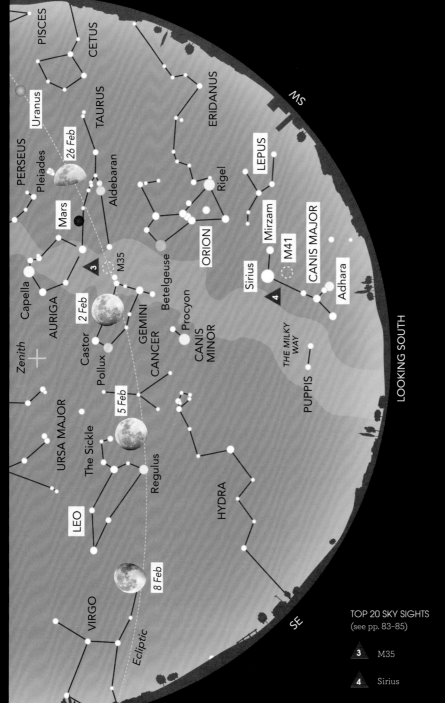

WEST

PISCES

CETUS

PERSEUS

Uranus

TAURUS

26 Feb

Pleiades

Mars

Aldebaran

ERIDANUS

Rigel

ORION

LEPUS

Betelgeuse

Mirzam

M41

CANIS MAJOR

Sirius

Adhara

M35

Capella

AURIGA

2 Feb

GEMINI

Castor

Pollux

CANCER

Procyon

CANIS MINOR

THE MILKY WAY

PUPPIS

Zenith

URSA MAJOR

5 Feb

The Sickle

Regulus

LEO

HYDRA

8 Feb

VIRGO

Ecliptic

3

4

S

SE

LOOKING SOUTH

TOP 20 SKY SIGHTS
(see pp. 83–85)

3   M35

4   Sirius

EAST

Venus, Jupiter and **Mars** are brilliant beacons in the evening sky, along with more A-lister stars than you'll see in any other month. **Orion** and his entourage are drifting to the west, while **Leo** (the Lion) and **Boötes** (the Herdsman) are rising higher in the east. That's because our perspective on the Universe is constantly changing as the Earth orbits the Sun.

FEBRUARY'S CONSTELLATION

Canis Major is the larger of **Orion's** two hunting dogs, and it's crowned by **Sirius** – the Dog Star – which is the brightest star in the sky. The Great Dog is chasing **Lepus** (the Hare), a faint constellation cowering below Orion.

To the right of Sirius lies **Mirzam**, whose Arabic name means 'the Announcer', because it rises just before Sirius. Prominent **Adhara** (magnitude +1.5) only just fails to make the list of first-magnitude stars. Five million years ago, Adhara was the most brilliant star in the sky as it passed close to the Sun, blazing as brightly as Venus.

The beautiful star cluster **M41** contains around a hundred young stars. It's easily visible through binoculars, and even to the unaided eye. The Greek philosopher Aristotle, in 325 BC, referred to 'a cloudy spot' in Canis Major: if that was M41 it's the earliest surviving description of a deep-sky object.

FEBRUARY'S OBJECT

A pair of objects this month: the beautiful **Double Cluster** in **Perseus**, on the border with **Cassiopeia**. Visible to the unaided eye, these near-twin star clusters – each covering an area bigger than the Full Moon – are a gorgeous sight in binoculars. Each cluster is loaded with glorious young, blue supergiant stars, with a sprinkling of red giants to add to their visual appeal.

The star cluster h Persei (otherwise known as NGC 869) is 7460 light years away from us, and chi Persei (NGC 884) is slightly further away at 7640 light years. They form the core of the Perseus OB1 Association, an extensive group of bright, hot stars that were born together 14 million years ago

FEBRUARY'S TOPIC: CHINESE ASTRONOMY

On 5 June 1302 BC, a Chinese scribe wrote: 'Three flames ate the Sun, and big stars were seen.' This account of a total eclipse of the Sun is the earliest astronomical record we have today.

The Chinese also meticulously observed at night, because they regarded the starry sky as a mirror of the Earth. A star erupting in a particular constellation portended an insurrection in the

---

OBSERVING TIP

Don't think that you need a telescope to bring the heavens closer. Binoculars are excellent – and you can fling them into the back of the car at the last minute. For astronomy, buy binoculars with large lenses coupled with a modest magnification. An ideal size is 7 × 50, meaning that the magnification is seven times, and that the diameter of the lenses is 50 mm.

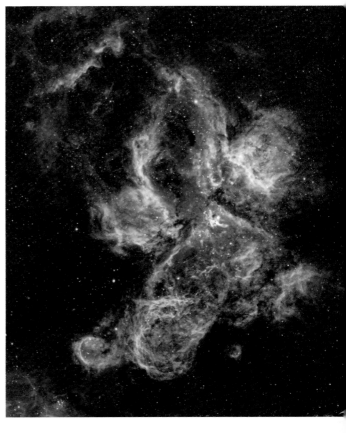

Pete Williamson observed remotely with a 106-mm f/5 Takahashi refractor located at the Siding Spring Observatory, New South Wales, Australia. Using an FLI camera, he took three 5 × 500-second shots, through filters passing light from silicon, hydrogen and oxygen atoms.

corresponding part of the Empire.

To complicate matters, the Chinese connected the stars into 283 small constellations – with names like the Court Eunuchs and the Sombre Axe – rather than the 88 largish star patterns that we use in the West. Only a few, like Orion, are identical. The familiar W-shape we see as Queen Cassiopeia, for instance, the Chinese split into three separate star patterns, one depicting a famous charioteer.

As well as eclipse records, the treasure trove of Chinese observations includes supernovae seen in AD 185, 1006, 1054 and 1181, and a whole panoply of comets, including the earliest record of Halley's Comet, as it crossed the sky in 240 BC.

FEBRUARY'S PICTURE

The great Carina Nebula is one of the most splendid sights in the night sky: four times larger than the more famous Orion Nebula and much brighter. It's often overlooked though, as it's too far south to be visible from the traditional home of astronomy in Europe and North America.

That didn't deter Pete Williamson, though. From his home in Shropshire, UK, he remotely controlled a telescope in New South Wales, Australia.

Near the centre of this image lies the powerhouse of the Carina Nebula: a compact cluster that includes some of the most massive and hottest stars in our entire Galaxy. The behemoth, Eta Carinae, is 100 times heavier than the Sun and shines 5 million times more brightly: it's destined to explode as a supernova in the near future.

SUNDAY	MONDAY	TUESDAY	WEDNESDAY	THURSDAY	FRIDAY	SATURDAY
			1	2	3 Moon near Castor and Pollux	4
5 6.29 pm Full Moon	6 Moon near Regulus	7	8	9	10 Moon near Spica	11
12	13 4.01 pm Last Quarter Moon	14	15 Moon near Antares (am); Venus near Neptune	16	17	18
19	20 7.06 am New Moon	21	22 Moon between Venus and Jupiter	23 Moon near Jupiter and Venus	24	25
26 Moon near Pleiades and Aldebaran	27 8.06 am First Quarter Moon near Mars and Aldebaran	28				

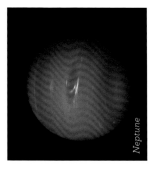

Neptune

SPECIAL EVENTS

• **15 February:** Venus passes very close to Neptune this evening. To identify the outermost planet, point your binoculars or small telescope towards Venus, and you'll find Neptune just 20 arcminutes to the lower right (Chart 2a). You're seeing the brightest and the dimmest planets in the same field of view, with Venus 60,000 times brighter than Neptune.

• **22 February:** there's a stunning sight to be seen in the west after sunset, with the crescent Moon lying between the two most brilliant planets, Venus and Jupiter (Chart 2b).

• **23 February:** you'll find Jupiter below the crescent Moon, with brighter Venus lower down towards the horizon.

• **27 February:** the First Quarter Moon lies close to Mars, with Aldebaran below.

2a *15 February, 7 pm. Venus very near Neptune (view through binoculars).*

2b *22 February, 7 pm. The crescent Moon between Venus and Jupiter.*

- **Venus** is spectacular after sunset, at magnitude –3.9, and setting about 8 pm. During February, the Evening Star heads inexorably upwards towards the second brightest planet, Jupiter. The Moon joins these two worlds on 22 February (see Special Events).

- Outermost planet **Neptune** (magnitude +7.9) lies in the same region of the sky – on the border of Aquarius and Pisces – and also sets around 8 pm. On 15 February, use Venus as a guide to spotting the outermost planet (see Special Events and Chart 2a).

- Brighter than any of the stars at magnitude –2.1, **Jupiter** is in Pisces and sets about 9 pm. The Moon passes by on 22 February, when Venus is also encroaching on the giant planet (Chart 2b).

- Lying in Aries, dim **Uranus** (magnitude +5.7) is setting around 1.30 am.

- **Mars** is among the stars of Taurus – to the left of the Pleiades – and sets about 3.30 am. At magnitude +0.1, the Red Planet is a little brighter than the constellation's principal star, the red giant Aldebaran. The Moon is nearby on 27 February.

- Look low in the south-east before sunrise, to spot **Mercury** during the first week of February. At magnitude –0.1, the innermost planet rises about 6.30 am.

- **Saturn** is too close to the Sun to be seen this month.

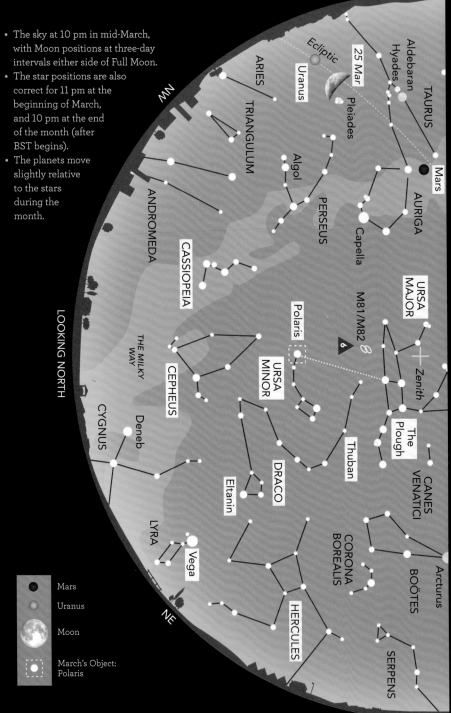

- The sky at 10 pm in mid-March, with Moon positions at three-day intervals either side of Full Moon.
- The star positions are also correct for 11 pm at the beginning of March, and 10 pm at the end of the month (after BST begins).
- The planets move slightly relative to the stars during the month.

LOOKING NORTH

WEST

NW

ARIES

TRIANGULUM

ANDROMEDA

Ecliptic

Uranus

25 Mar

Pleiades

Hyades

Aldebaran

TAURUS

Mars

AURIGA

Algol

PERSEUS

Capella

CASSIOPEIA

M81/M82

URSA MAJOR

THE MILKY WAY

Polaris

6

Zenith

CEPHEUS

URSA MINOR

The Plough

Deneb

CYGNUS

DRACO

Thuban

CANES VENATICI

Eltanin

LYRA

Vega

HERCULES

CORONA BOREALIS

BOÖTES

Arcturus

NE

SERPENS

Mars

Uranus

Moon

March's Object: Polaris

20 MARCH

EAST

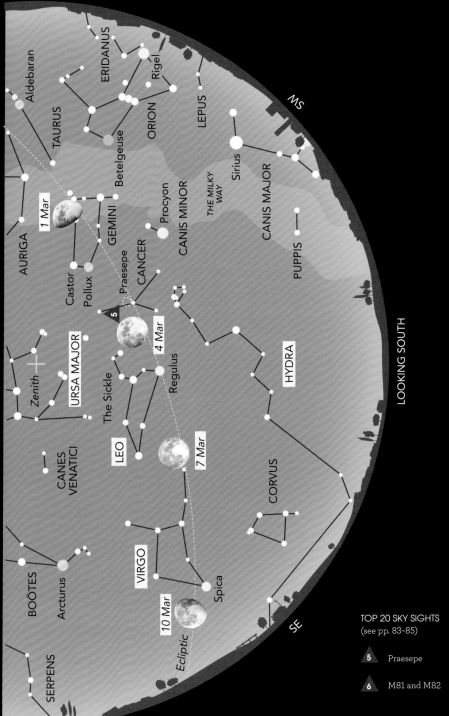

WEST

MS

Aldebaran
ERIDANUS
TAURUS
Rigel
ORION
Betelgeuse
GEMINI
LEPUS
Sirius
THE MILKY WAY
CANIS MAJOR
AURIGA
1 Mar
Castor
Pollux
Praesepe
CANCER
Procyon
CANIS MINOR
PUPPIS
Zenith
URSA MAJOR
5
4 Mar
The Sickle
Regulus
HYDRA
CANES VENATICI
LEO
7 Mar
CORVUS
BOÖTES
Arcturus
VIRGO
Spica
10 Mar
Ecliptic
SERPENS

SE

LOOKING SOUTH

TOP 20 SKY SIGHTS
(see pp. 83–85)

5 Praesepe

6 M81 and M82

MARCH   **21**

EAST

Don't miss a spectacular tango involving Venus and Jupiter right at the start of the month. The large spring constellations **Leo**, **Virgo** and **Hydra** are now well on view in the southern sky. And we shouldn't forget the northern constellations that are visible every night of the year: Queen **Cassiopeia** and her consort **Cepheus**, **Draco** (the Dragon), and the two Bears – **Ursa Major** and **Ursa Minor**.

MARCH'S CONSTELLATION

The cosmic dragon writhes between the two bears in the northern sky. In Greek myth, **Draco** was slain by **Hercules** in his mission to steal golden apples from a sacred grove.

Eltanin, in the dragon's head, is an orange star 154 light years away, shining at magnitude +2.2. But in 1.5 million years' time, it will dash past the Earth at just 28 light years, blazing as the brightest star in our skies.

At first sight, **Thuban** seems an unassuming star, at mere magnitude +3.7. But what Thuban lacks in brightness, it makes up for in fame. Thuban was the Pole Star at the time the Great Pyramids were built in Egypt, in the third millennium BC. That's because the Earth's axis gradually swings around in space – rather like the toppling of a spinning top – over a period of 26,000 years. At the moment, our planet's axis points to Polaris (see Object), but in 2800 BC it was lined up with Thuban. Come AD 14,000, it will be brilliant **Vega**'s turn to be our North Star.

MARCH'S OBJECT

The Pole Star, or North Star, is so well known that many people expect it to be among the brightest stars in the sky. In fact, **Polaris** (to use its official name) is surprisingly modest: at magnitude +2.0,

it's the same brightness as the stars making up the **Plough**, and you can use the end stars of the Plough to locate the Pole Star (see Star Chart).

Its fame rests on the fact that Polaris just happens to lie above the Earth's North Pole, so our planet rotates underneath it. As a result, this star remains almost stationary in the sky, due north wherever or whenever you observe it. Its constant position makes the Pole Star an essential guide for navigators.

Polaris lies at the end of the tail of the Little Bear (**Ursa Minor**). It's a massive yellow star, five times heavier than the Sun and 1200 times brighter. As it swells and shrinks regularly, the North Star's brightness varies slightly over a period of four days.

OBSERVING TIP

This is the ideal time of year to tie down the main compass directions, as seen from your observing site. North is easy – just latch onto Polaris, the Pole Star, using the familiar stars of the Plough (see Object). And at noon, the Sun is always in the south. But the useful extra in March is that we hit the Spring Equinox, when the Sun rises due east, and sets due west. So remember those positions relative to a tree or house around your horizon.

MARCH'S TOPIC: SETI

It's the biggest question in astronomy: is there anybody out there? Over 60 years ago, American astronomer Frank Drake kick-started the Search for Extraterrestrial Intelligence (SETI) when he turned his radio telescope to the heavens in the hope of hearing an alien broadcast. He was met with a deafening silence.

Since then, astronomers have used ever more sensitive instruments to tune into the sky, including the world's largest telescope at Arecibo in Puerto Rico (before it collapsed in 2020) and a purpose-built array of dishes in California.

Others have tried to pick up flashes of laser light from other civilisations. Researchers have checked whether unusual-looking stars may be surrounded by giant structures built by aliens. And there's a search for extraterrestrial spacecraft speeding through the Galaxy.

So far, all to no avail. Maybe the aliens are using technology far beyond our comprehension? Or they may be intentionally minimising contact with us, to observe our primitive ways, as we monitor

animals in the wild. Or, most sobering of all, perhaps we are the only intelligent life form in our Galaxy.

MARCH'S PICTURE

This fiery blaze of light is a solar prominence, soaring thousands of kilometres above the edge of the Sun. Prominences appear above groups of sunspots, and are a sensational sign of our local star's magnetic activity. You can see prominences at a total eclipse of the Sun, or through specialised photographic equipment, as captured here by Gary Palmer.

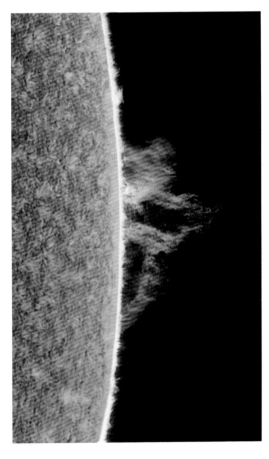

From Rhayader in Wales, Gary Palmer imaged this solar prominence on 10 October 2018. His telescope was a Starwave 115-mm EDT fitted with a DayStar Quark Chromosphere solar filter, and the camera an Altair GP-CAM 290M USB3. Gary used SharpCap Pro capture software and processed the image in AS!2 and Photoshop C56.

SUNDAY	MONDAY	TUESDAY	WEDNESDAY	THURSDAY	FRIDAY	SATURDAY
			1 Venus very near Jupiter	2 Moon near Castor and Pollux	3	4
5 Moon near Regulus	6	7 12.40 pm Full Moon	8	9 Moon near Spica	10 Moon near Spica	11
12	13	14 Moon near Antares (am)	15 2.08 am Last Quarter Moon	16	17	18
19	20 Spring Equinox	21 5.23 pm New Moon	22	23 Moon between Jupiter and Venus	24 Moon near Venus	25 Moon near Pleiades
26 BST begins; Moon near Aldebaran	27	28 Moon near Mars	29 3.32 am First Quarter Moon near Castor and Pollux	30 Moon near Castor and Pollux	31	

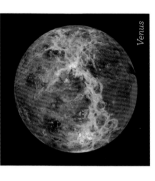

Venus

SPECIAL EVENTS

- **1 March:** the two brightest planets have a very close encounter this evening when Venus skims past Jupiter (see Planet Watch and Chart 3a).
- **20 March, 9.24 pm:** the Spring Equinox, when day and night are of equal length.
- **23 March:** check out the magnificent alignment of Venus (top), the crescent Moon (middle) and Jupiter (lowest) in the evening twilight (Chart 3b).
- **24 March:** the crescent Moon pairs up with Venus, the brilliant Evening Star, to create a stunning celestial duo (Chart 3b).
- **26 March, 1.00 am:** British Summer Time starts – don't forget to put your clocks forward.
- **28 March:** the Moon lies next to Mars.

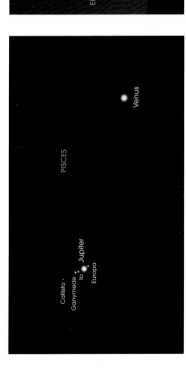

3a 1 March, 7 pm. Venus passes Jupiter, with its brightest moons (view through binoculars).

Callisto ·
Ganymede ·
Io · Jupiter
Europa

PISCES

Venus

TAURUS

24 Mar

Venus

ANDROMEDA

ARIES

23 Mar

Jupiter

PEGASUS

ERIDANUS

CETUS

PISCES

WSW   W   WNW

3b 23-24 March, 7.15 pm. The crescent Moon with Jupiter and Venus.

• Low in the west after sunset, the month opens with the stunning sight of the two most brilliant planets up close and personal.

• Dominating the scene is **Venus**, at a magnificent magnitude –4.0. On 1 March, it's only 35 arcminutes from **Jupiter** (Chart 3a). At magnitude –2.1, the giant planet is five times fainter than the Evening Star.

• The planetary pair sinks below the horizon around 8.30 pm. As the month progresses, Jupiter – in Pisces – drops down into the twilight glow and it's lost to sight by the end of the month.

• Meanwhile, Venus rises ever higher into the darker night-time sky. By the close of March, the Evening Star doesn't set until 11 pm.

The Moon lies nearby on 23 and 24 March (Chart 3b).

• Towards the end of the month, Venus is in the vicinity of **Uranus**. The dim seventh planet (magnitude +5.8) lies in Aries and also sets about 11 pm.

• You'll find **Mars** lying in Taurus, at magnitude +0.7, fading all the time as it heads towards Gemini. The Red Planet sets around

2.30 am. The Moon is nearby on 28 March.

• **Mercury, Saturn** and **Neptune** are lost in the Sun's glare during March.

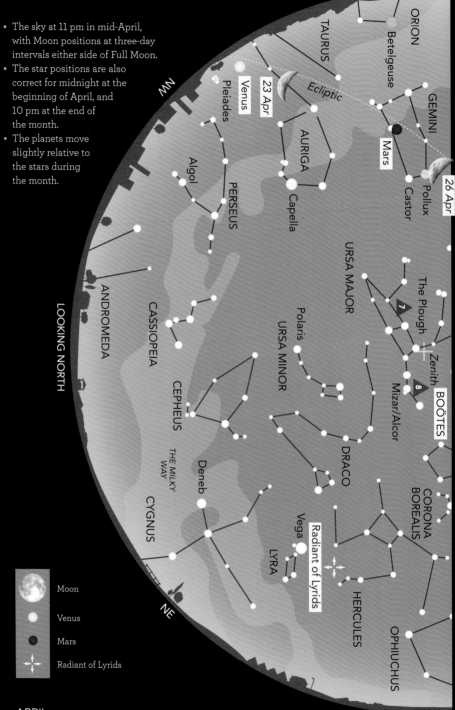

- The sky at 11 pm in mid-April, with Moon positions at three-day intervals either side of Full Moon.
- The star positions are also correct for midnight at the beginning of April, and 10 pm at the end of the month.
- The planets move slightly relative to the stars during the month.

WEST

ORION
Betelgeuse
TAURUS
GEMINI
Ecliptic
23 Apr
Venus
Pleiades
Mars
Pollux
Castor
26 Apr
AURIGA
Algol
Capella
PERSEUS
URSA MAJOR
Capella
The Plough
Zenith
Mizar/Alcor
BOÖTES
ANDROMEDA
CASSIOPEIA
Polaris
URSA MINOR
CORONA BOREALIS
LOOKING NORTH
CEPHEUS
DRACO
THE MILKY WAY
Deneb
Vega
Radiant of Lyrids
HERCULES
CYGNUS
LYRA
OPHIUCHUS
NE

Moon
Venus
Mars
Radiant of Lyrids

EAST

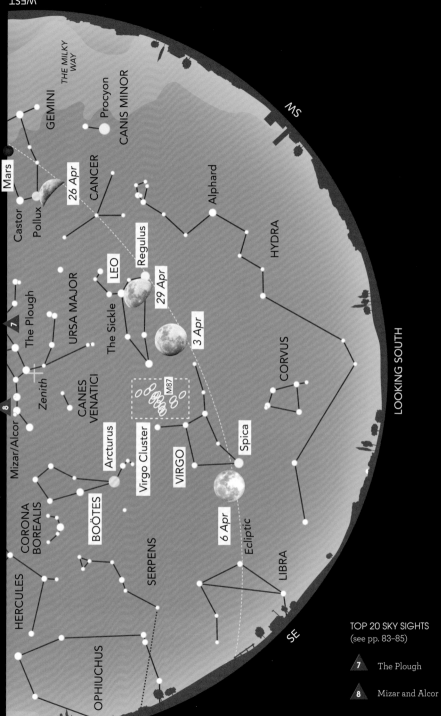

WEST

EAST

THE MILKY WAY

GEMINI

Procyon

CANIS MINOR

Mars

Castor

Pollux

26 Apr

CANCER

Regulus

LEO

29 Apr

The Sickle

3 Apr

URSA MAJOR

The Plough

7

8

Mizar/Alcor

Zenith

CANES VENATICI

Arcturus

Virgo Cluster

M87

VIRGO

Spica

6 Apr

Ecliptic

BOÖTES

CORONA BOREALIS

HERCULES

SERPENS

LIBRA

OPHIUCHUS

Alphard

HYDRA

CORVUS

SW

MS

LOOKING SOUTH

SE

TOP 20 SKY SIGHTS
(see pp. 83–85)

7   The Plough

8   Mizar and Alcor

All three of our nearest neighbour planets are well on view in the evening sky – Mercury, **Venus** and **Mars**. And three bright stars ride high this month, dominating the major constellations of the spring skies. Leading the way is **Regulus** in **Leo**, with **Virgo**'s leading star **Spica** to the lower left, and orange **Arcturus** in **Boötes** lying above.

APRIL'S CONSTELLATION

The Y-shaped constellation of **Virgo** is the second largest in the sky. Traditionally this pattern represents a virtuous maiden holding an ear of corn (the bright star **Spica**), because the Sun passed through Virgo at harvest time.

Spica is a hot, blue-white star over 20,000 times brighter than the Sun, with a temperature of 25,000°C. It has a stellar companion, which circles Spica more closely than Mercury orbits the Sun. The stars inflict a mighty gravitational toll on each other, stretching each star out into an egg shape.

The glory of Virgo lies in the 'bowl' of the Y-shape. Scan the upper region with a small telescope – at a low magnification – and you'll find it packed with faint, fuzzy blobs. These are just a few of the 2000 galaxies that make up the gigantic **Virgo Cluster**. It's centred on the mammoth galaxy **M87**, which boasts a central black hole over 6 billion times heavier than the Sun: it was the first black hole to be imaged, in 2019.

APRIL'S OBJECT

This month is your best chance to spot tiny **Mercury** during the evening (see Planet Watch). The innermost planet of the Solar System, Mercury never strays far from the Sun in the sky. Whizzing round its tiny oval-shaped orbit, Mercury completes one 'year' in just 88 Earth days. The planet is spinning on its axis so slowly that it takes a whole Mercury year for the Sun to cross the sky from sunrise to sunset.

Only a little bigger than our Moon, Mercury too is covered in craters. But that's where the resemblance ends. Mercury has a huge core made of molten iron. As the core cooled, the planet has shrunk, wrinkling its surface like the skin of a dried-up apple.

Paradoxically, astronomers have found that this scorched world has patches of ice, deep in craters at Mercury's poles where sunlight never penetrates. Here, future colonists could live on Mercury, obtaining power from solar panels high on the sun-drenched mountains, and drawing life-giving water from the ice on the crater floors.

OBSERVING TIP

Venus is glorious this month. Through a small telescope, you can make out its cloud-wreathed globe, half-lit by the Sun. But don't wait for the sky to get totally dark. Seen against a black sky, Venus is so brilliant it's difficult to discern any details. You're best off viewing Venus soon after the Sun has set, when the Evening Star first becomes visible in the twilight glow. Through a telescope, the planet then appears less dazzling against a pale blue sky.

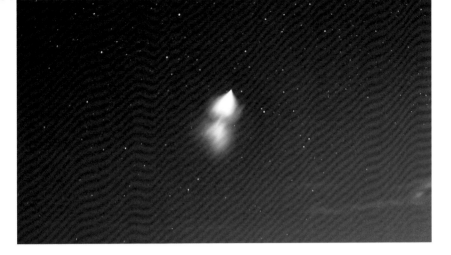

APRIL'S TOPIC: HENRIETTA LEAVITT

Though she made a breakthrough cosmic discovery, American astronomer Henrietta Swan Leavitt (1868–1921) never used a telescope. Instead, she looked downwards through a magnifying glass, studying photographic plates of the sky taken by colleagues in Peru.

Comparing plates taken at different times, she found thousands of stars that changed in brightness: one colleague called her 'a variable-star fiend'. In 1912, Leavitt analysed 25 cepheid variable stars (named after Delta Cephei – see May's Object) in a prominent swarm of stars called the Small Magellanic Cloud, and realised that the more luminous a cepheid is, the longer the period from maximum light, through minimum and back to maximum again.

It was a staggering breakthrough. Measure the period of a cepheid anywhere in the Universe, and 'Leavitt's Law' tells you instantly how luminous it is. Compare that to its apparent brightness, dimmed by distance, and you can work out how far away the star lies.

In the 1920s, astronomers used Leavitt's discovery to prove the existence of

From Buckie in Scotland, Kieran MacGregor was looking across the Moray Firth when he captured this rocket plume. He used a Nikon D7500 camera and Sigma 14-mm f/2.8 lens, with a 10-second exposure at ISO 1250.

galaxies beyond our own Milky Way – such as the Andromeda Galaxy – and then to show that the Universe is expanding.

APRIL'S PICTURE

When astronomers are up all night, they get used to seeing strange flashes and lights in the sky, such as shooting stars and aurorae. But what on Earth – or off Earth – was this glowing double jellyfish that Kieran MacGregor spotted moving across the heavens in September 2021?

No, it wasn't a UFO. It was indeed a spacecraft, but not an alien one. This was the exhaust plume from the upper stage of an Atlas V rocket, which had taken off from the Vandenberg Air Force Base in California and placed the Landsat 9 Earth-observation satellite into orbit. Now – as it passed over Britain – the Centaur stage turned round and reignited its rocket engine, slowing it down so it fell back into the atmosphere and safely burnt up. The manoeuvre was designed to reduce space junk orbiting the Earth.

SUNDAY	MONDAY	TUESDAY	WEDNESDAY	THURSDAY	FRIDAY	SATURDAY
30						1
2 Moon near Regulus	3 Moon near Regulus	4	5	6 5.34 am Full Moon near Spica	7	8
9	10 Moon near Antares (am)	11 Mercury E elongation; Venus near Pleiades	12	13 10.11 am Last Quarter Moon	14	15
16 Moon near Saturn (am)	17	18	19	20 5.12 am New Moon; hybrid solar eclipse	21	22 Moon between Venus and Pleiades; Lyrids
23 Lyrids (morning); Moon near Venus	24	25 Moon near Mars	26 Moon near Castor and Pollux	27 10.20 pm First Quarter Moon	28	29 Moon near Regulus

SPECIAL EVENTS

- **11 April:** the Pleiades lie just to the right of brilliant Venus (Chart 4a).
- **16 April, before dawn:** Saturn lies immediately above the crescent Moon.
- **20 April:** parts of Western Australia and Indonesia are treated to a strange beast of a solar eclipse. It starts in the Indian Ocean as an annular eclipse, where a thin band of the Sun's surface is visible around the Moon's silhouette. At mid-eclipse – visible from East Timor – the eclipse becomes total; and then over the Pacific it's back to an annular eclipse. A partial eclipse is visible from all of Australia, Indonesia and the Philippines. Nothing of this hybrid eclipse is visible from Europe or North America.
- **22 April:** a thin crescent Moon lies to the lower right of brilliant Venus; further down towards the horizon you may spot the Pleiades.
- **Night of 22/23 April:** it's an excellent year for observing the maximum of the **Lyrid meteor shower**, as the Moon is well out of the way. These shooting stars appear to emanate from the constellation Lyra as debris from Comet Thatcher burns up in the Earth's atmosphere, and they often leave glowing trails of dust.
- **23 April:** Venus hangs just below the crescent Moon, in a stunning twilight pairing.
- **25 April:** the Moon lies near Mars, beneath Castor and Pollux (Chart 4b).

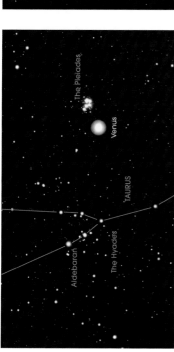

4a *11 April, 9 pm. Venus passes the Pleiades, near Aldebaran and the Hyades.*

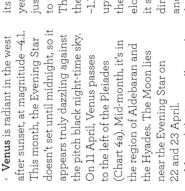

4b *25 April, 10 pm. The Moon close to Mars, in Gemini.*

- **Venus** is radiant in the west after sunset, at magnitude –4.1. This month, the Evening Star doesn't set until midnight, so it appears truly dazzling against the pitch black night-time sky. On 11 April, Venus passes to the left of the Pleiades (Chart 4a). Mid-month, it's in the region of Aldebaran and the Hyades. The Moon lies near the Evening Star on 22 and 23 April.

- Meanwhile, its smaller and fainter sibling is putting on its best evening show of the year. You can find **Mercury** just above the horizon, well to the lower right of Venus. The innermost planet starts the month at magnitude –1.1, but it fades as it moves upwards into darker skies. By the time it reaches maximum elongation on 11 April – when it sets at 10 pm – Mercury has dimmed to magnitude +0.1; and it fades from sight as it drops into the twilight by the third week of April.

- **Uranus** is not far from Mercury, in Aries, and also sets around 10 pm. But being much fainter, at a mere magnitude +5.8, the seventh planet is difficult to spot and it too disappears into the dusk glow in the second half of April.

- **Mars** (magnitude +1.2) lies in Gemini, and sets about 2.30 am. The Moon is nearby on 25 April (Chart 4b). By the end of the month, the Red Planet is approaching Castor and Pollux, all three about the same brightness.

- In the morning sky, you'll find **Saturn** rising around 5 am, moving upwards in the sky as the month progresses. The ringed planet lies in Aquarius, and shines at magnitude +1.0. The Moon is nearby on the morning of 16 April.

- **Jupiter** and **Neptune** are too close to the Sun to be seen this month.

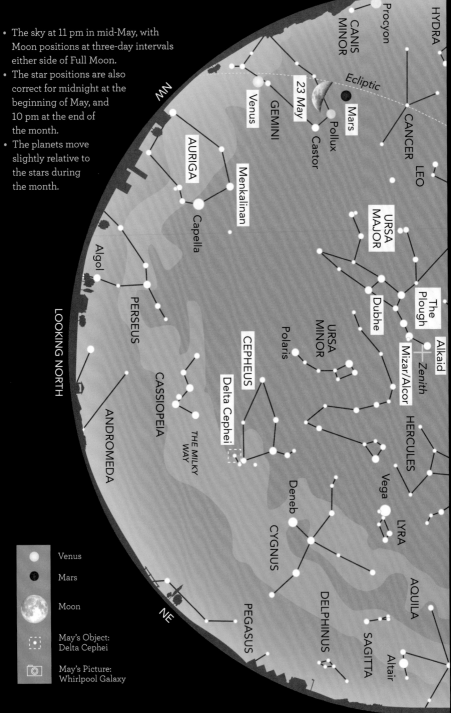

- The sky at 11 pm in mid-May, with Moon positions at three-day intervals either side of Full Moon.
- The star positions are also correct for midnight at the beginning of May, and 10 pm at the end of the month.
- The planets move slightly relative to the stars during the month.

WEST

HYDRA

CANIS MINOR

Procyon

Ecliptic

NW

Venus

23 May

CANCER

LEO

GEMINI

Pollux

Castor

Mars

AURIGA

Menkalinan

URSA MAJOR

Capella

The Plough

Dubhe

Alkaid

Algol

PERSEUS

CEPHEUS

Polaris

URSA MINOR

Mizar/Alcor

Zenith

HERCULES

LOOKING NORTH

CASSIOPEIA

Delta Cephei

THE MILKY WAY

Vega

LYRA

ANDROMEDA

Deneb

CYGNUS

AQUILA

NE

PEGASUS

DELPHINUS

SAGITTA

Altair

Venus

Mars

Moon

May's Object: Delta Cephei

May's Picture: Whirlpool Galaxy

MAY

EAST

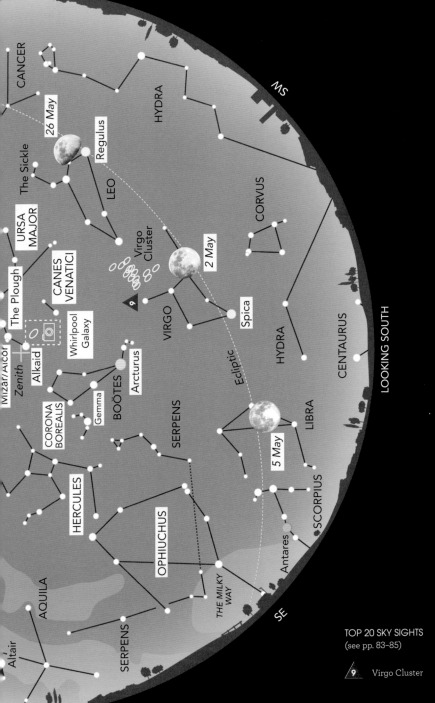

MAY

WS

CANCER

HYDRA

26 May

The Sickle

Regulus

LEO

URSA
MAJOR

CORVUS

The Plough

CANES
VENATICI

Virgo
Cluster

2 May

Mizar/Alcor

Zenith

Whirlpool
Galaxy

Alkaid

VIRGO

Spica

9

Arcturus

BOÖTES

Ecliptic

HYDRA

CENTAURUS

SERPENS

CORONA
BOREALIS

Gemma

LIBRA

5 May

LOOKING SOUTH

HERCULES

OPHIUCHUS

SCORPIUS

AQUILA

THE MILKY
WAY

Antares

SE

Altair

SERPENS

TOP 20 SKY SIGHTS
(see pp. 83–85)

9 Virgo Cluster

MAY   **33**

Venus and Mars grace the western sky, while the southern part of the heavens is dominated by the brilliant orange star **Arcturus**. Well to its lower right, you'll find the bright blue-white stars **Spica** and **Regulus**. But the region to the left of Arcturus boasts only the faint stars of two giant constellations, **Ophiuchus** and **Hercules**.

MAY'S CONSTELLATION

Ursa Major, the Great Bear, is an internationally favourite constellation. In Britain and Ireland, its seven brightest stars are called the **Plough**, though children today often call it 'the saucepan'. In North America, it's known as the Big Dipper. Always on view in the northern hemisphere, the Plough is the first star pattern that most people get to know.

Look closely at the star in the middle of the bear's tail (or the handle of the saucepan), you'll see it's double. **Mizar** and its fainter companion **Alcor** comprise one of the few binary stars you can 'split' with unaided eye.

And – unlike most constellations – the majority of the stars in the Plough lie at the same distance and were born together. Leaving aside **Dubhe** and **Alkaid**, the others are all moving in the same direction, along with other stars of the Ursa Major Moving Group, which include **Menkalinan** in **Auriga** and **Gemma** in **Corona Borealis**. Over thousands of years, the shape of the Plough will gradually change, as Dubhe and Alkaid go off on their own paths.

MAY'S OBJECT

At first glance, the star **Delta Cephei** – in the constellation representing King **Cepheus** – seems pretty ordinary. At magnitude +4, this yellow star is visible to the naked eye, though it's not prominent. A telescope reveals a companion

star. But Delta Cephei holds the key to measuring the size of the Universe.

Check Delta Cephei carefully, and you'll see its brightness changes regularly, from +3.5 to +4.4, every 5 days 9 hours. It's a result of the star swelling and shrinking, from 40 to 45 times the Sun's diameter.

The American astronomer Henrietta Leavitt (see April's Topic) found that stars like this – cepheids – show a link between their period of variation and their intrinsic luminosity. By observing the star's period and its apparent brightness, astronomers can work out a cepheid's distance. With the Hubble Space Telescope, astronomers have now measured cepheids in NGC 4603, a remote galaxy 107 million light years away.

MAY'S TOPIC: GALAXIES

Sweep the May sky around Virgo, Leo and Ursa Major with binoculars on a really dark night, and you'll stumble over

Jean Dean, observing in Guernsey, captured the Whirlpool Galaxy with a William Optics FLT132 refracting telescope and Starlight Xpress Trius 814 mono CCD camera, through LRGB and H-alpha filters. The total integration time was 2 hours 40 minutes.

dozens of faint fuzzy patches, each a galaxy consisting of billions of stars (many of them lie in the Virgo Cluster, the featured Top Sky Sight this month – see page 83).

Galaxies come in three basic types. Some are stately spiral galaxies like our Milky Way or the Whirlpool Galaxy (see Picture). These are rich in gas and dust, poised to make new generations of stars, and adorned with beautiful curving arms made of young, hot stars.

Irregular galaxies have a similar mix of ingredients, but are smaller and lack any distinctive shape: the Small Magellanic Cloud, visible from the southern hemisphere is a good example.

Elliptical galaxies range from very small to truly gargantuan, but they are all boringly oval in shape. Most of their stars are old and red; there's very little gas and dust in these galaxies to make new stars. But there's sometimes action in the centre of an elliptical galaxy, where powerful jets of energy are shooting out from the vicinity of a central black hole.

MAY'S PICTURE

The stunning **Whirlpool Galaxy** (M51) is always a draw for astrophotographers, and you can see why in this spectacular image by Jean Dean. The Whirlpool – and its companion, NGC 5195 – grace the tiny constellation of **Canes Venatici**. Lying 28 million light years away, the Whirlpool is small but perfectly formed. It's only half the width of our Milky Way galaxy, and one-tenth as massive, but its prominent whorls mean it was the first galaxy recognised as a spiral, way back in 1845.

Some 500 million years ago, NGC 5195 passed through its larger companion, pulling out streamers of gas, and triggering a massive episode of starbirth. The heaviest young stars are exploding as supernovae: three have been observed in the past 30 years.

SUNDAY	MONDAY	TUESDAY	WEDNESDAY	THURSDAY	FRIDAY	SATURDAY
	1	2	3 Moon near Spica	4	5 6.34 pm Full Moon	6
7 Eta Aquarids (am); Moon near Antares	8	9	10	11	12 3.28 pm Last Quarter Moon	13 Moon near Saturn (am)
14 Moon near Saturn (am)	15	16	17 Moon near Jupiter (am)	18	19 4.53 pm New Moon	20
21	22 Moon near Venus	23 Moon near Venus, Castor and Pollux	24 Moon near Mars	25	26 Moon near Regulus	27 4.22 pm First Quarter Moon
28	29 Mercury W elongation	30	31 Moon near Spica; Venus near Castor and Pollux			

Crescent Moon

SPECIAL EVENTS

- **Morning of 7 May:** the annual Eta Aquarid meteor shower – tiny pieces of Halley's Comet burning up in Earth's atmosphere – is predicted to be unusually intense this year, but, sadly, bright moonlight will spoil the show.

- **13–14 May, before dawn:** the crescent Moon passes below Saturn (Chart 5a).

- **22 May:** the thin crescent Moon hangs to the lower right of the brilliant Evening Star, Venus (Chart 5b).

- **23 May:** Venus and the crescent Moon are up close and personal in the twilight sky; Castor and Pollux are just above, with Mars off to the left (Chart 5b).

- **24 May:** Mars lies below the crescent Moon, with Castor, Pollux and Venus to the lower right (Chart 5b).

5a 13-14 May, 4 am. The waning Moon sails under Saturn.

5b 22-24 May, 11 pm. The crescent Moon passes Venus and Mars.

• The Evening Star blazes in the west as the month begins, not setting until after midnight. At magnitude –4.2, **Venus** is far brighter than anything else in the evening sky except the Moon. Find a really dark spot, away from streetlights and moonlight, let your eyes adapt to the dark (see Observing Tip) – and you may be able to make out shadows cast by the Evening Star. The Moon forms a striking pair with Venus on

22 and 23 May (see Special Events and Chart 5b).

• **Mars** lies well to the upper left of Venus, firmly put into the shade by its flashier sibling: the Red Planet glows at magnitude +1.5, almost 200 times fainter than the Evening Star, and sets about 1.30 am. Starting the month in Gemini, Mars speeds past Castor and Pollux around 10 May. Crossing into Cancer, the planet has a close encounter with the Moon

on 24 May (see Special Events and Chart 5b).

• The sky is then devoid of planets, until **Saturn** rises around 3 am. Lying in Aquarius, the ringworld shines at magnitude +1.0. The Moon is nearby on the mornings of 13 and 14 May (Chart 5a).

• **Neptune** is rising about 3.30 am, in Pisces. The outermost planet is at magnitude +7.9.

• Last, but far from least, on this month's roster of

planets is mighty **Jupiter**, which reappears low in the morning sky in mid-May. The planet rises around 4 am, and shines brightly on the border of Pisces and Aries, at magnitude –2.1. The crescent Moon is nearby on the morning of 17 May.

• **Uranus** and **Mercury** are both lost in the Sun's glare this month, even though the innermost planet reaches greatest separation from the Sun on 29 May.

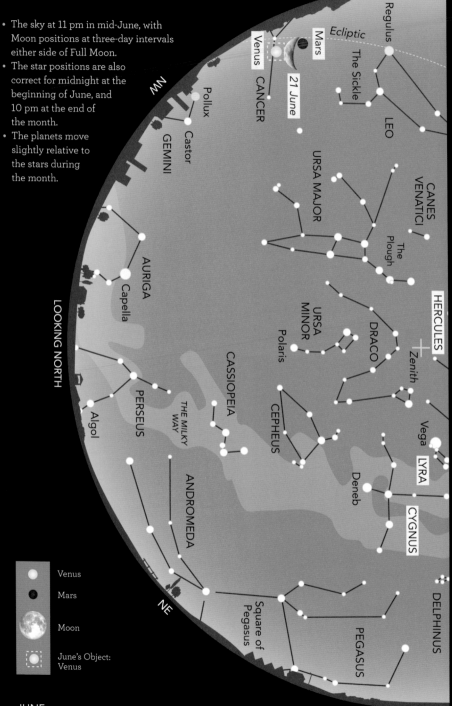

- The sky at 11 pm in mid-June, with Moon positions at three-day intervals either side of Full Moon.
- The star positions are also correct for midnight at the beginning of June, and 10 pm at the end of the month.
- The planets move slightly relative to the stars during the month.

WEST

Regulus

Ecliptic

Mars

Venus

The Sickle

CANCER

21 June

LEO

NW

Pollux

GEMINI

Castor

CANES VENATICI

URSA MAJOR

The Plough

HERCULES

AURIGA

Capella

URSA MINOR

Polaris

DRACO

Zenith

LOOKING NORTH

CASSIOPEIA

Vega

PERSEUS

THE MILKY WAY

CEPHEUS

LYRA

Algol

Deneb

CYGNUS

ANDROMEDA

Venus

Mars

Moon

June's Object: Venus

Square of Pegasus

PEGASUS

DELPHINUS

NE

JUNE

EAST

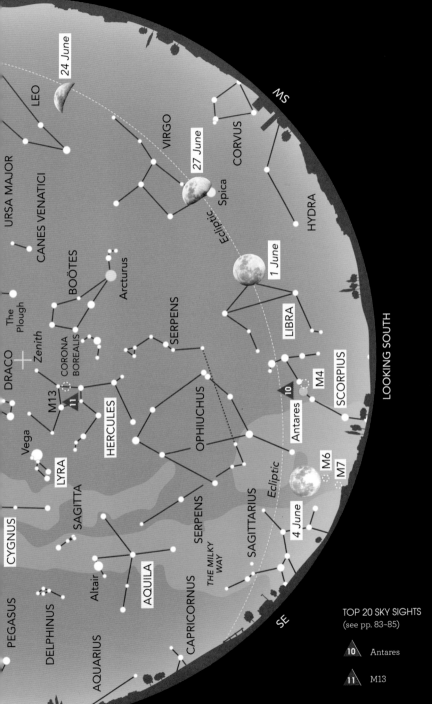

WEST

SW

JUNE

24 June

LEO

URSA MAJOR

CANES VENATICI

VIRGO

27 June

CORVUS

BOÖTES

Arcturus

Spica

Ecliptic

HYDRA

The Plough

Zenith

SERPENS

1 June

DRACO

CORONA BOREALIS

LIBRA

LOOKING SOUTH

M13

11

Vega

OPHIUCHUS

Antares

SCORPIUS

M4

10

HERCULES

M6

LYRA

4 June

M7

SAGITTA

Ecliptic

CYGNUS

SERPENS

SAGITTARIUS

THE MILKY WAY

PEGASUS

Altair

AQUILA

CAPRICORNUS

SE

DELPHINUS

AQUARIUS

TOP 20 SKY SIGHTS
(see pp. 83-85)

10 Antares

11 M13

JUNE   **39**

EAST

Though the sky never quite grows dark this month – especially for the northern regions of Britain – take advantage of the warm nights to enjoy the lovely summer constellations of **Hercules, Scorpius, Lyra, Cygnus** and **Aquila**. And watch **Venus** and **Mars** as they encounter the star cluster known as the Beehive.

JUNE'S CONSTELLATION

Down in the deep south of the sky lies a baleful red star. **Antares**, meaning 'the rival of Mars', surpasses in ruddiness even the famed Red Planet. To the ancient Greeks, Antares marked the heart of **Scorpius**, the scorpion that killed the apparently invincible hunter Orion. The gods placed both in the sky, but at opposite sides, so Orion sets as Scorpius rises.

Unusually, Scorpius resembles its terrestrial namesake. A line of stars to the top right of Antares marks the scorpion's forelimbs. Originally, the stars we now call **Libra** (the Scales) were its claws. Below Antares, the scorpion's body stretches down into a fine curved tail (below the horizon on the Star Chart) and deadly sting.

Scorpius is a treasure trove of astronomical goodies. Several lovely double stars include Antares: its faint companion looks greenish in contrast to Antares's strong red hue. Binoculars reveal the fuzzy patch of **M4**, a globular cluster made of tens of thousands of stars, some 7200 light years away. Above the 'sting' lie two gorgeous star clusters – **M6** and **M7** – visible to the naked eye when they're well above the horizon: a telescope reveals their stars clearly.

JUNE'S OBJECT

Venus – the planet of love – is resplendent in our evening skies this month. Its pure lantern-like luminosity is beguiling. But looks are deceptive. Though Earth's twin in size, Venus could hardly be more different from our warm, wet world.

Venus is entirely draped in highly reflective clouds, but – unlike our friendly water clouds – Venus's all-enveloping pall is made of drops of concentrated sulphuric acid. They hang in an atmosphere of unbreathable carbon dioxide, so dense that the atmospheric pressure at its surface is 90 Earth atmospheres. This thick blanket of carbon dioxide traps the Sun's heat, creating a runaway Greenhouse Effect that has made Venus the hottest planet in the Solar System: at 460°C, it's far hotter than an oven.

OBSERVING TIP

June is a great month for observing the Sun, with our local star at its highest in the sky. But NEVER look at the Sun directly, with your unprotected eyes or – especially – with a telescope or binoculars: it could blind you permanently. For naked-eye observing, use special 'eclipse glasses' with dark filters (meeting the ISO 12312-2 safety standard). You can project the Sun's image through binoculars or a telescope onto a piece of white card; or attach a filter made of special material (such as Baader AstroSolar® film) across the front of the instrument. Best of all – though not cheap – acquire a solar telescope with built-in filters for safely observing details of the Sun's churning surface.

The surface bristles with 1600 major volcanoes, and perhaps as many as a million smaller volcanoes. Any way you look at it, seductive Venus is the planet from Hell!

JUNE'S TOPIC: SOLAR CYCLE

In the early nineteenth century, German amateur astronomer Heinrich Schwabe (1789–1875) carefully watched dark spots on the Sun every day for 17 years, thinking he might see an unknown planet pass across its face. Becoming intrigued by the sunspots themselves, he discovered that their number rises, and then falls again, over a period of 11 years.

The culprit is the Sun's magnetic field. It's generated in the turbulent gases that lie within our local star, and generally threads its way around the Sun below its surface. But the Sun's equator spins around faster than the gas at its poles, and so the magnetic field is stretched out like a rubber band – until something has to give . . .

Like a writhing piece of elastic, the magnetism breaks out through the surface. Where it erupts, the magnetic field locally quenches its brilliance, producing a dark sunspot. The pent-up energy creates more and more of these dark blemishes for several years, building up to sunspot maximum, when we may see a hundred sunspots simultaneously. Eventually, the magnetic field – and the sunspots – die away again. At sunspot minimum, weeks may go past without any spots appearing on the Sun's face.

Max Alexander caught this sunrise during the week of the 2008 Summer Solstice at Stonehenge, with a Nikon D3 camera, equipped with a 300-mm Nikon lens and ×2 teleconverter. The exposure was 1/40 second at f/16 and ISO 200.

The latest solar cycle began in December 2019, and sunspot numbers are rising. We expect solar maximum around July 2025.

JUNE'S PICTURE

The Summer Solstice conjures up images of Stonehenge with Sun worshippers staying up all night to watch out for sunrise – as beautifully captured in Max Alexander's atmospheric image of the Sun rising over the ancient stones.

Recent archaeological research has confirmed our ancestors did assemble from all around the country to celebrate the solstice at this atmospheric site – but it wasn't in the summer, but at the Midwinter Solstice in December, when they observed the Sun setting behind the monument. Whatever the time of year, though, Stonehenge and the Sun together evoke a deep emotional resonance in us.

SUNDAY	MONDAY	TUESDAY	WEDNESDAY	THURSDAY	FRIDAY	SATURDAY
				1 ◐	2 Mars in Praesepe ○	3 Moon very close to Antares ○
4 4.42 am Full Moon; Venus E elongation ○	5 ○	6 ○	7 ○	8 ◐	9 ◐	10 8.31 pm Last Quarter Moon near Saturn (am) ◐
11 ◐	12 ◐	13 Venus very close to Praesepe ◐	14 Moon very near Jupiter (am) ◐	15 ◐	16 ◐	17 ◐
18 5.37 am New Moon ●	19 ●	20 ●	21 Summer Solstice; Moon near Venus and Mars ◐	22 Moon near Mars, Venus and Regulus ◐	23 Moon near Regulus ◐	24 ◐
25 ◐	26 8.50 am First Quarter Moon ◐	27 Moon very near Spica ◐	28 ○	29 ○	30 Moon near Antares ○	

SPECIAL EVENTS

- **2 June:** Mars lies right in the middle of the star cluster Praesepe: though it's low in the evening sky, it's a great sight in binoculars or a small telescope.
- **3 June:** a few hours before it's Full, the Moon skims just above the bright red giant Antares (Chart 6a).

Praesepe

- **13 June:** Venus passes just above Praesepe.
- **14 June:** Jupiter lies next to the thin crescent Moon, low in the morning twilight.
- **21 June, 3.57 pm:** Summer Solstice. The Sun reaches its most northerly point in the sky, so today is Midsummer's Day, with the longest daylight period and the shortest night.

- **21 June:** the thin crescent Moon pairs up with Venus in a beautiful twilight spectacle, with Mars lying to the left (Chart 6b).
- **22 June:** Venus lies to the right of the crescent Moon; in between you'll find fainter Mars, with Regulus to the left of the Moon.

6a 3 June, 11.30 pm. The Full Moon very close to Antares.

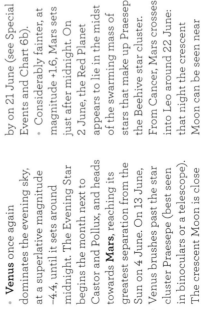

6b 21 June, 11 pm. The crescent Moon with Venus and Mars.

Venus once again dominates the evening sky, at a superlative magnitude −4.4, until it sets around midnight. The Evening Star begins the month next to Castor and Pollux, and heads towards **Mars**, reaching its greatest separation from the Sun on 4 June. On 13 June, Venus brushes past the star cluster Praesepe (best seen in binoculars or a telescope). The crescent Moon is close

by on 21 June (see Special Events and Chart 6b).

• Considerably fainter, at magnitude +1.6, Mars sets just after midnight. On 2 June, the Red Planet appears to lie in the midst of the swarming mass of stars that make up Praesepe, the Beehive star cluster. From Cancer, Mars crosses into Leo around 22 June: that night the crescent Moon can be seen near

the Red Planet (see Special Events).

• The next planet on the celestial stage is **Saturn**, rising about 1 am. The ringed planet lies in Aquarius, shining at magnitude +0.9. The Moon is nearby on the morning of 10 June.

• **Neptune** (magnitude +7.9), in Pisces, rises around 1.30 am.

• Clearing the horizon about 3.30 am, **Jupiter** is king of

the morning sky at a glorious magnitude −2.2. The giant planet is in Aries, and the crescent Moon is right next to it on the morning of 14 June.

• **Uranus** reappears in the morning sky in the last few days of June, rising about 2.30 am. It shines dimly in Aries, at magnitude +5.8.

• **Mercury** is too close to the Sun to be visible in June.

- The sky at 11 pm in mid-July, with Moon positions at three-day intervals either side of Full Moon.
- The star positions are also correct for midnight at the beginning of July, and 10 pm at the end of the month.
- The planets move slightly relative to the stars during the month.

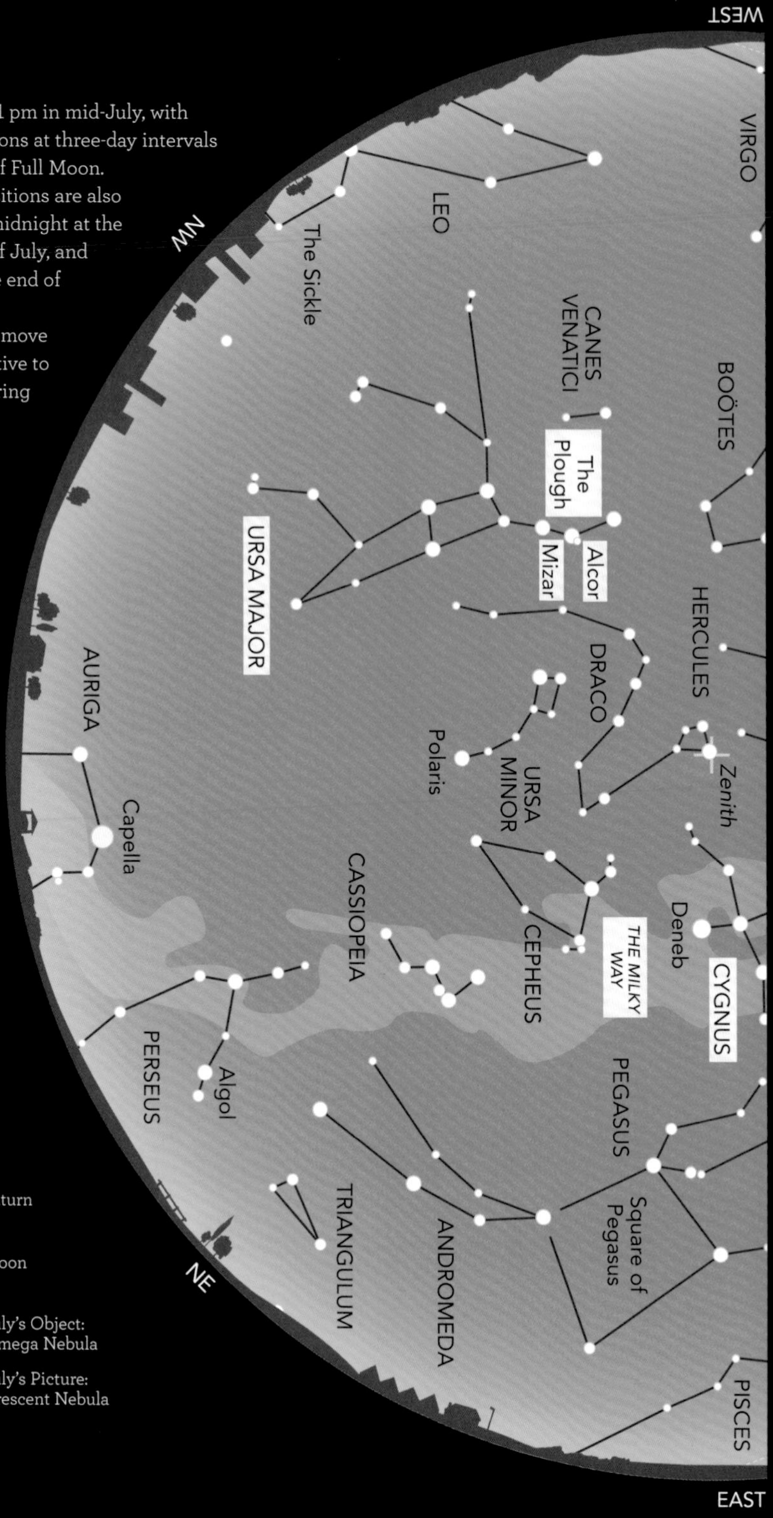

WEST

VIRGO

LEO

CANES VENATICI

BOÖTES

The Sickle

NW

The Plough

HERCULES

URSA MAJOR

Mizar

Alcor

DRACO

AURIGA

Polaris

URSA MINOR

Zenith

Capella

LOOKING NORTH

CASSIOPEIA

CEPHEUS

THE MILKY WAY

Deneb

CYGNUS

PERSEUS

Algol

TRIANGULUM

ANDROMEDA

PEGASUS

Square of Pegasus

NE

PISCES

Saturn

Moon

July's Object: Omega Nebula

July's Picture: Crescent Nebula

JULY

EAST

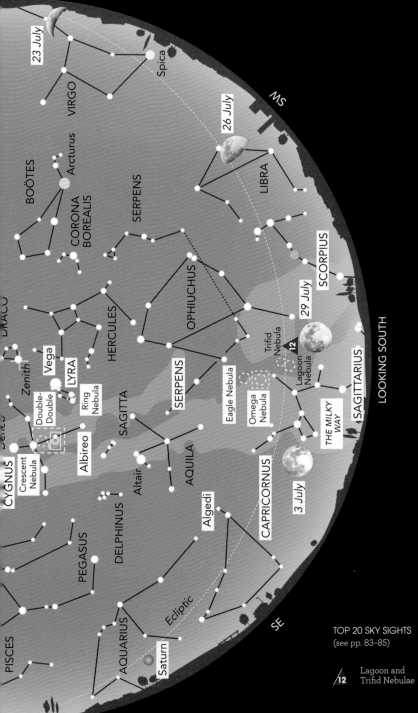

WEST

23 July

Spica

VIRGO

26 July

Arcturus

BOÖTES

CORONA
BOREALIS

SERPENS

LIBRA

DRACO

HERCULES

OPHIUCHUS

SCORPIUS

29 July

Vega

Zenith

LYRA

Ring
Nebula

Double-
Double

Albireo

SAGITTA

SERPENS

Eagle Nebula

Omega
Nebula

Trifid
Nebula

12

Lagoon
Nebula

SAGITTARIUS

THE MILKY
WAY

LOOKING SOUTH

SW

CYGNUS

Crescent
Nebula

Altair

AQUILA

CAPRICORNUS

3 July

PEGASUS

DELPHINUS

Algedi

PISCES

AQUARIUS

Saturn

Ecliptic

SE

Venus has been with us since last December, but this month it's suddenly gone! Before it sinks into the evening twilight, watch its celestial waltz with Mars, Mercury and the Moon. Also, two ancient constellations are at their best this month, **Sagittarius** and **Scorpius**, decorating the southern region of the sky against the background of the **Milky Way**.

JULY'S CONSTELLATION

Lyra is small but perfectly formed. Shaped like a Greek lyre, it's dominated by brilliant white **Vega**, the fifth-brightest star in the sky. Just 25 light years away, Vega is surrounded by a disc of dust and gas, probably the debris from the destruction of comets or asteroids orbiting the star.

Next to Vega is the **Double-Double**, a quadruple star known officially as epsilon Lyrae. Keen-sighted people can separate the pair, and a small telescope reveals each star is itself double.

The gem of Lyra lies between the two stars at the base of the lyre, though you'll need a telescope to observe the **Ring Nebula**: it's faint (magnitude +9) and only a little larger than Jupiter in apparent size. This is a wonderful example of a planetary nebula, named by William Herschel because these objects look a bit like the planet Uranus he had just discovered. But in reality the Ring Nebula is a ghostly star corpse, the ejected atmosphere of a star that has reached the end of its life.

JULY'S OBJECT

The **Omega Nebula** – in Sagittarius – is an overlooked twin. Close by in **Serpens**, the **Eagle Nebula** is famous because it contains the iconic Pillars of Creation snapped by the Hubble Space Telescope. The Omega Nebula is equally bright

(magnitude +6.0), and a striking sight in a small telescope.

In 1823, John Herschel compared the nebula to the Greek letter Omega (Ω), though only one horizontal bar is visible and the loop is faint. Charles Messier, listing the nebula as number 17 in his 1781 catalogue, saw only the bar, and described it as 'a train of light without stars'.

And that's what makes the Omega Nebula so unusual. When we look at most nebulae (such as the Orion or Lagoon Nebulae), they appear bright largely because our eyes are also taking in light from a central cluster of stars. While there is a star cluster associated with the Omega, it's hidden by a dark dust cloud within the loop. So the Omega Nebula is among the brightest clouds of purely luminous gas that we can see in the sky.

JULY'S TOPIC: DOUBLE STARS

The Sun is an exception in living a solitary life. Over half the stars you see in the sky are paired up, as double stars. In some cases, it's just that a distant star happens to lie almost behind a nearer one. To the naked eye, **Algedi** in **Capricornus** looks double, but the fainter star lies nine times further off than the brighter component.

The most famous celestial double act lies in the **Plough** in **Ursa Major**. **Mizar** (the brighter star) and its fainter companion **Alcor** have often been named 'the horse and rider'. These two stars are travelling together through space.

Most double stars, though, are orbiting each other – astronomers call them binary stars. Check out the star marking the head of **Cygnus** (the Swan), **Albireo**, with a small telescope and you're in for a treat: a golden star with a sapphire companion. Often, the stars are so close that astronomers have known they are double only by examining their light in detail, and seeing evidence of two stars moving alternately towards and away from us.

And binary stars are just the first step. The Double-Double in Lyra is exactly what its name proclaims: two pairs of stars in orbit around each other (see Constellation). Castor, one of the twin stars of Gemini, consists of three pairs of binary stars – making it a sextuple star.

JULY'S PICTURE

Cygnus is filled with the red glow of hydrogen gas lit by hot young stars, but here Sara Wager has captured the dying throes of a star about to exit the cosmic scene, energising a strange cosmic jellyfish.

The **Crescent Nebula** (NGC 6888) is centred on a massive star, 21 times heavier than the Sun. The star has ripped through its nuclear fuel in only a few million years, and is now unstable, blasting off its outer layers into space and exposing the super-hot nuclear reactor at the star's core, at a searing 70,000°C. The expelled shell of gas, now 25 light years across, is visible as the Crescent Nebula.

Using a 250-mm f/6.8 Orion Optics ODK10 telescope equipped with a QSI 683 camera, Sara Wager shot the Crescent Nebula through several different filters: H-alpha (50 × 30 minutes), OIII (51 × 30 minutes) and a Baader RGB set (15 × 5 minutes through each filter). The total exposure time was 54 hours 15 minutes!

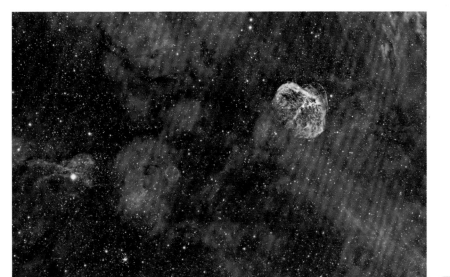

SUNDAY	MONDAY	TUESDAY	WEDNESDAY	THURSDAY	FRIDAY	SATURDAY
30	31					1 Moon near Antares
2	3 12.39 pm Full Moon, supermoon	4	5	6 Earth at aphelion; Moon near Saturn	7	8
9 Venus at maximum brightness	10 2.48 am Last Quarter Moon	11	12 Moon near Jupiter (am)	13	14 Moon near Pleiades and Aldebaran (am)	15
16	17 7.32 pm New Moon	18	19 Moon near Venus, Mercury, Regulus and Mars	20 Moon near Venus, Mars, Regulus and Mercury	21	22
23	24 Moon near Spica	25 11.07 pm First Quarter Moon	26	27	28 Moon near Antares	29

Supermoon

SPECIAL EVENTS

- **3 July:** the first of four supermoons this year – see August for more details.
- **6 July, 9.07 pm:** the Earth is furthest from the Sun (aphelion), at 152 million km.
- **9 July:** Venus reaches its greatest brilliance as an Evening Star, at magnitude –4.5.
- **12 July, before dawn:** bright Jupiter lies right next to the crescent Moon (Chart 7a).
- **19 July:** the thinnest crescent Moon hangs to the right of brilliant Venus, low in the west after sunset (Chart 7b). With binoculars, pick out Mercury below the Moon, and Regulus and Mars above Venus.
- **20 July:** Venus lies below the Moon, with Regulus in between, Mars to the left and Mercury to the right (Chart 7b) – binoculars will help.

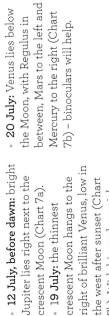

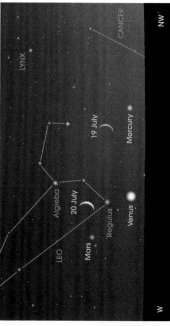

7a 12 July, 2.30 am. The Moon close to Jupiter.

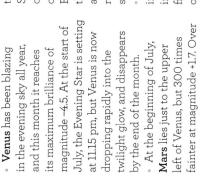

7b 19–20 July, 9.45 pm. The crescent Moon with Mercury, Venus and Mars.

Venus has been blazing in the evening sky all year, and this month it reaches its maximum brilliance of magnitude –4.5. At the start of July, the Evening Star is setting at 11.15 pm, but Venus is now dropping rapidly into the twilight glow, and disappears by the end of the month.

At the beginning of July, Mars lies just to the upper left of Venus, but 300 times fainter at magnitude +1.7. Over the past months, the Evening Star has been moving steadily closer to Mars, and when July opens they are just 3.5° apart. But as Venus drops towards the horizon, Mars heads up and away. The Red Planet remains in Leo all month, and sets about 11 pm.

These two worlds are joined in the latter half of July by the innermost planet. Mercury first appears to the lower right of Venus about 15 July, at magnitude –0.6 and setting around 10 pm. On 19 and 20 July, the thin crescent Moon joins the three planets and Regulus low in twilight – a lovely sight best viewed in binoculars (Chart 7b).

As these planets set, over to the east Saturn is rising about 11 pm. The sixth planet lies in Aquarius, and shines at magnitude +0.7. The Moon passes just below Saturn on the night of 6 July.

Faint Neptune lies in the neighbouring constellation of Pisces. Mustering a magnitude of only +7.8, the outermost world rises about 11.30 pm.

Jupiter, in Aries, is rising around 1 am, shining gloriously, at magnitude –2.3. The Moon is very nearby in the early hours of 12 July (Chart 7a).

Also in Aries, Uranus follows Jupiter over the horizon about 1.30 am. It's borderline naked-eye visibility, at magnitude +5.8.

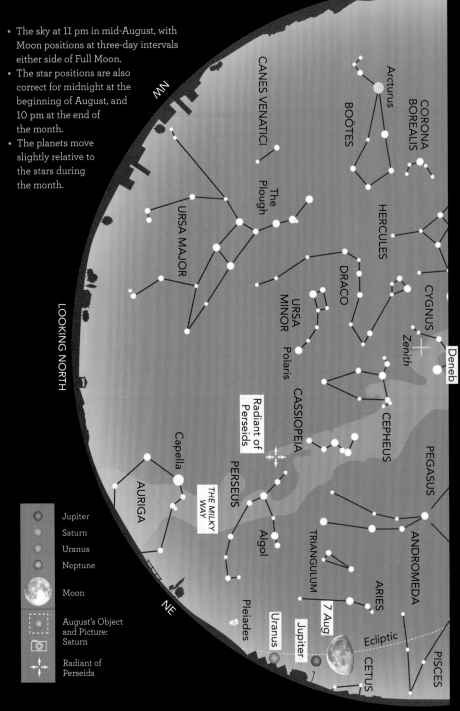

- The sky at 11 pm in mid-August, with Moon positions at three-day intervals either side of Full Moon.
- The star positions are also correct for midnight at the beginning of August, and 10 pm at the end of the month.
- The planets move slightly relative to the stars during the month.

WEST

NW

CANES VENATICI

The Plough

BOÖTES

Arcturus

CORONA BOREALIS

HERCULES

URSA MAJOR

DRACO

CYGNUS

Zenith

Deneb

URSA MINOR

Polaris

CEPHEUS

LOOKING NORTH

Radiant of Perseids

CASSIOPEIA

PEGASUS

Capella

PERSEUS

THE MILKY WAY

AURIGA

Algol

TRIANGULUM

ANDROMEDA

Jupiter
Saturn
Uranus
Neptune

Moon

August's Object and Picture: Saturn

Radiant of Perseids

NE

Pleiades

Uranus

Jupiter

7 Aug

ARIES

Ecliptic

CETUS

PISCES

AUGUST

EAST

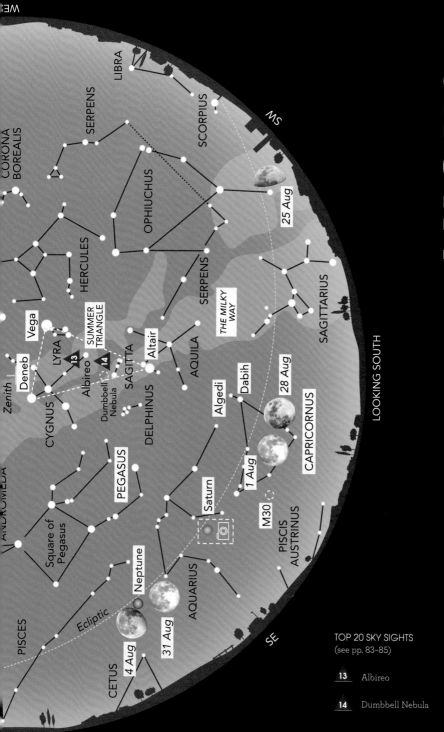

WEST

EAST

LIBRA

CORONA
BOREALIS

SERPENS

SCORPIUS

SW

OPHIUCHUS

HERCULES

SERPENS

25 Aug

SAGITTARIUS

Vega

SUMMER
TRIANGLE

THE MILKY
WAY

Deneb

LYRA

13

Albireo

14

Altair

Zenith

Dumbbell
Nebula

SAGITTA

AQUILA

CYGNUS

DELPHINUS

Algedi

Dabih

28 Aug

ANDROMEDA

PEGASUS

Saturn

1 Aug

CAPRICORNUS

Square of
Pegasus

M30

PISCIS
AUSTRINUS

LOOKING SOUTH

PISCES

Ecliptic

Neptune

AQUARIUS

CETUS

4 Aug

31 Aug

SE

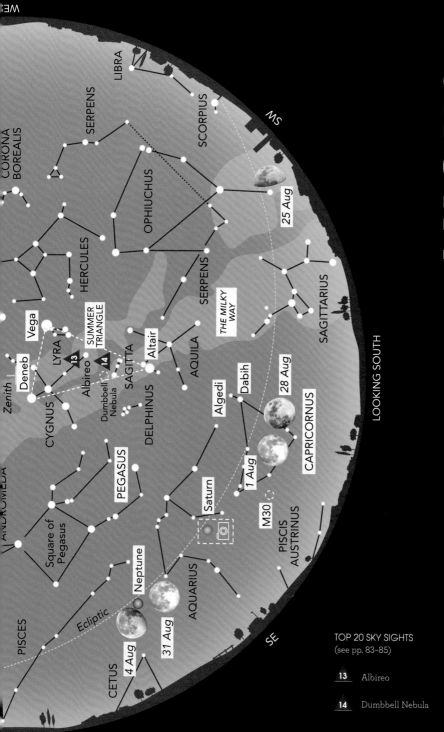

The **Milky Way** arches overhead this month, looking ever more resplendent as the skies grow darker. Set against its glowing band, three brilliant stars – **Vega**, **Deneb** and **Altair** – mark out the vertices of the **Summer Triangle**. We're treated to two supermoons this month, the second being the brightest Full Moon of the year. Also, look out for **Saturn** at its best and a spectacular display of the **Perseid meteor shower**.

AUGUST'S CONSTELLATION

Capricornus (the Sea Goat) is one of the faint, watery constellations below **Pegasus**, its triangular outline looking like a boat. The ancient Sumerians associated these stars with their great deity, Enki, who presided over both the sea and the creation of life – and so was represented as a strange being who was half-fish and half-goat.

Even with the unaided eye, you can see that **Algedi** is double. The two stars (magnitudes +3.6 and +4.3) aren't actually related, though, but happen to lie one behind the other (see July's Topic).

The next-door star **Dabih** is a genuine binary. The brighter member is a yellow star of magnitude +3.1; binoculars or a small telescope will reveal a blue companion at magnitude +6.1.

You can spot the globular cluster **M30** in binoculars, and a telescope reveals its swarming stars. This eighth-magnitude star cluster, about 27,000 light years away, orbits the opposite way to our Galaxy's rotation, so the smart money says

On 27 July 2020, just a week after Saturn was at opposition, Damian Peach captured the magnificence of its rings with a 500-mm f/15 Cassegrain telescope and an ASI290MM camera.

the Milky Way purloined M30 from a passing galaxy.

AUGUST'S OBJECT

Glorious ringworld **Saturn** takes centre stage in the heavens this month, reaching opposition on 27 August, and at its highest in the south at midnight. After Jupiter, Saturn is the second-largest planet. But its density is so low that – were you to plop it in an ocean – Saturn would float. The planet spins around in only 10 hours 33 minutes, whipping up winds that roar around Saturn at 1800 kilometres per hour.

The planet is famed for its huge engirdling appendages: Saturn's rings would stretch nearly all the way from the Earth to the Moon, and are thinner in proportion than a sheet of paper (see Picture).

And, of any planet, Saturn has the largest family of moons: 83 at the last count. The largest, Titan, is bigger than the planet Mercury and boasts lakes of liquid methane and ethane under a thick, cloudy atmosphere. The icy moon Enceladus is spewing salty water into space, while Dione has traces of oxygen in its thin atmosphere. These discoveries raise the intriguing possibility of primitive life on Saturn's moons . . .

AUGUST'S TOPIC: PERSEIDS

There's nothing more romantic on your summer holiday than wishing on a shooting star – except for experiencing a whole shower of meteors! So book your holiday somewhere with warm nights, and in the middle of August.

Every year, around 12 August, the Earth runs into a stream of debris shed by Comet Swift-Tuttle. The specks of cosmic dust (about the size of coffee granules)

smash into our atmosphere at a speed of 210,000 kilometres per hour, and burn up in the flash of glory that we call a meteor.

Because of perspective, these shooting stars all appear to diverge from the same part of the sky – the radiant – which lies in the constellation Perseus. Although it's an annual event, this month is a great time for viewing the **Perseids** as the show is not spoilt by moonlight. Stay up late on 12 August for guaranteed celestial fireworks!

AUGUST'S PICTURE

Saturn is a glorious sight through a small telescope: it looks surreal, like a finely crafted model dangling against a black background. And its rings – stunningly captured here by Damian Peach three years ago – are among the most spectacular of all astronomical sights.

Saturn's rings consist of over a trillion ice particles, individually orbiting the planet as 'mini-moons' around a metre in size. Damian's image clearly shows the Cassini Division, a dark gap in the rings where the icy chunks have been swept clear by the gravity of Saturn's moons.

SUNDAY	MONDAY	TUESDAY	WEDNESDAY	THURSDAY	FRIDAY	SATURDAY
		1 7.31 pm Full Moon, supermoon	**2** Moon near Saturn	**3** Moon near Saturn	**4**	**5**
6	**7**	**8** 11.28 am Last Quarter Moon; Moon near Jupiter (am)	**9** Moon between Jupiter and Pleiades (am)	**10** Moon near Aldebaran (am); Mercury E elongation	**11**	**12** Perseids
13 Perseids (am)	**14**	**15**	**16** 10.38 am New Moon	**17**	**18** Moon near Mars and Mercury	**19**
20	**21** Moon near Spica	**22**	**23**	**24** 10.57 am First Quarter Moon near Antares	**25**	**26**
27 Saturn opposition	**28**	**29**	**30** Moon near Saturn	**31** 2.35 am Full Moon, supermoon		

SPECIAL EVENTS

- **1 August:** there's a bright supermoon tonight, just a tad less prominent than the month's second supermoon – see 31 August.
- **8 August, early hours:** Jupiter hangs right next to the Moon.
- **9 August, early hours:** the Moon lies between the Pleiades and Jupiter (Chart 8a).
- **10 August, early hours:** the star below the Moon is Aldebaran, with the Pleiades to the upper right.
- **Night of 12/13 August:** maximum of the **Perseid meteor shower.** It's an excellent year for observing one of the year's most prolific displays of shooting stars – high-speed pellets of dust from comet Swift-Tuttle

burning up high above our heads (see Topic).
- **18 August:** with the help of binoculars, you'll find Mars just to the left of the narrow crescent Moon, and Mercury below in the twilight glow.
- **27 August:** Saturn is opposite to the Sun in the sky, and closest to the Earth at a distance of 1311 million km (see Planet Watch).

- **31 August:** in the early hours of the morning, the Moon is at its most brilliant this year, lying close to Saturn (Chart 8b). But don't expect to be blinded by the light: this supermoon is only 30% brighter than the faintest Full Moon. As the second Full Moon of the month, it will be hailed as the 'blue supermoon' – but don't expect it to appear azure either!

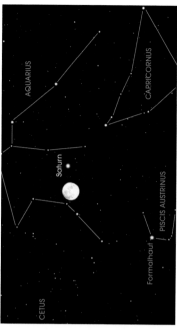

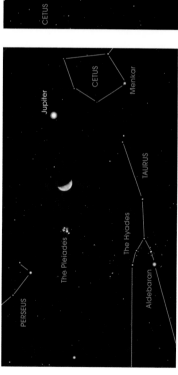

8a *9 August, 3 am. The Moon between the Pleiades and Jupiter.*

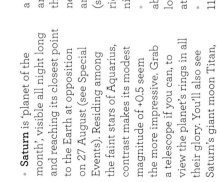

8b *31 August, 2.35 am. The brightest Full Moon of the year lies next to Saturn.*

• **Saturn** is 'planet of the month', visible all night long and reaching its closest point to the Earth at opposition on 27 August (see Special Events). Residing among the faint stars of Aquarius, contrast makes its modest magnitude of +0.5 seem the more impressive. Grab a telescope if you can, to view the planet's rings in all their glory. You'll also see Saturn's giant moon Titan, a satellite so massive it has an atmosphere denser than the Earth's air. The Moon is nearby on 2 and 3 August; and the 'blue supermoon' (see Special Events) sails right under Saturn on the night of 30/31 August.

• Nearby **Neptune** is also above the horizon all night, located in Pisces and shining at magnitude +7.8.

• **Jupiter** is rising about 11 pm, in Aries. It dominates the rest of night sky, at a brilliant magnitude –2.5. The Moon is nearby in the morning skies of 8 and 9 August (Chart 8a).

• Not far to the left of the giant planet, **Uranus** lies in Aries, on the boundary with Taurus. The seventh planet rises around 11 pm, and shines at magnitude +5.7.

• **Venus** reappears in the dawn sky in the last week of August. Rising about 5 am, the Morning Star is resplendent at magnitude –4.2.

• **Mercury** and **Mars** are lost in the Sun's glare this month, even though Mercury is at its greatest separation from the Sun on 10 August.

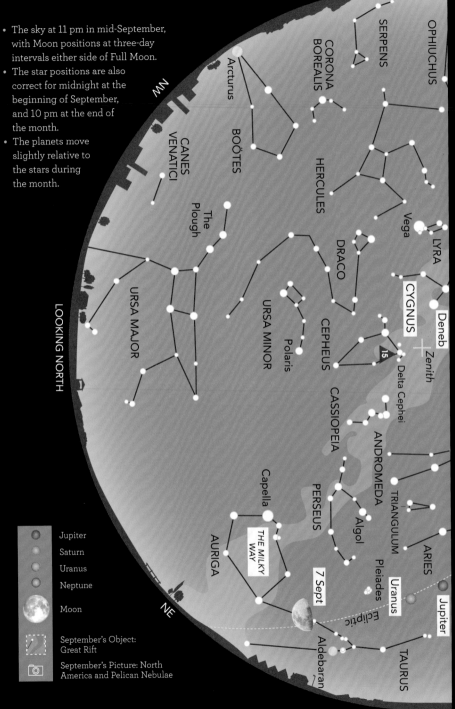

- The sky at 11 pm in mid-September, with Moon positions at three-day intervals either side of Full Moon.
- The star positions are also correct for midnight at the beginning of September, and 10 pm at the end of the month.
- The planets move slightly relative to the stars during the month.

WEST

LOOKING NORTH

NW

Arcturus

CORONA BOREALIS

SERPENS

OPHIUCHUS

CANES VENATICI

BOÖTES

HERCULES

Vega

LYRA

The Plough

DRACO

CYGNUS

Deneb

URSA MAJOR

URSA MINOR

CEPHEUS

Zenith

Delta Cephei

15

Polaris

CASSIOPEIA

ANDROMEDA

TRIANGULUM

Capella

PERSEUS

Algol

ARIES

AURIGA

THE MILKY WAY

7 Sept

Pleiades

Uranus

Jupiter

Ecliptic

Aldebaran

TAURUS

NE

Jupiter

Saturn

Uranus

Neptune

Moon

September's Object: Great Rift

September's Picture: North America and Pelican Nebulae

SEPTEMBER

EAST

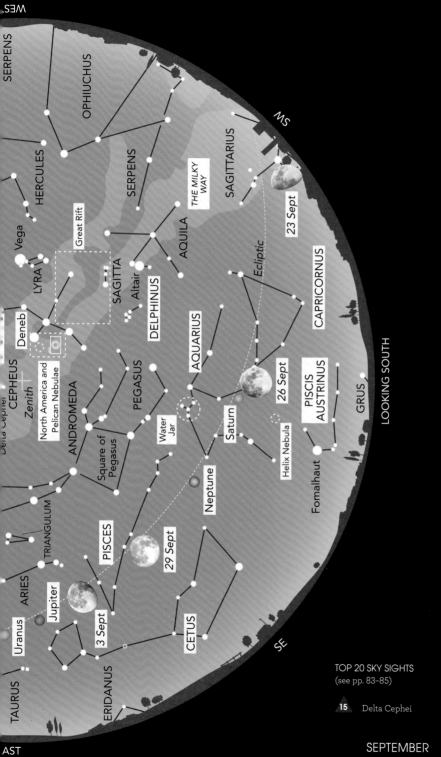

WEST

SERPENS

OPHIUCHUS

HERCULES

Vega

Great Rift

LYRA

Deneb

CEPHEUS

Zenith

North America and Pelican Nebulae

ANDROMEDA

Square of Pegasus

PEGASUS

TRIANGULUM

ARIES

TAURUS

Uranus

Jupiter

3 Sept

ERIDANUS

PISCES

29 Sept

CETUS

Neptune

SE

SERPENS

SAGITTA

Altair

DELPHINUS

AQUILA

AQUARIUS

Water Jar

Saturn

SW

SAGITTARIUS

THE MILKY WAY

23 Sept

Ecliptic

CAPRICORNUS

26 Sept

PISCIS AUSTRINUS

Helix Nebula

GRUS

Fomalhaut

LOOKING SOUTH

SEPTEMBER

TOP 20 SKY SIGHTS
(see pp. 83–85)

15 Delta Cephei

EAST

As summer ends with the arrival of the equinox, the southern sky is awash with the watery constellations of autumn. **Piscis Austrinus** (the Southern Fish) wallows in a fluid stream poured by **Aquarius** (the Water Carrier); they are surrounded by **Delphinus** (the Dolphin), the strangely named Sea Goat (**Capricornus**), a pair of Fishes (**Pisces**) and **Cetus** (the Sea Monster).

SEPTEMBER'S CONSTELLATION

Although hardly one of the most spectacular constellations, **Aquarius** (the Water Carrier) has a pedigree stretching back to antiquity. The ancient Babylonians associated this zone of the heavens with water because the Sun passed through it during the rainy season. The Greeks depicted Aquarius as a man pouring from a **Water Jar** (the central group of four faint stars), with the liquid splashing downwards onto **Piscis Austrinus** (the Southern Fish).

Aquarius boasts one of the most glorious sky sights in long-exposure images, though it's faint when viewed through binoculars or a small telescope. Half the diameter of the Full Moon, the **Helix Nebula** is a 'planetary nebula'– so-called because it resembles a faint version of Jupiter or Uranus – and, at 650 light years away, it's one of the nearest. In reality, the Helix is a star suffering its death throes. An aged red giant star has puffed off its distended atmosphere to form a beautiful shroud around its collapsed core, a white dwarf star that will gradually fade away to a cold, black cinder.

SEPTEMBER'S OBJECT

This month I'm picking out not a spectacular star cluster or nebula, but a region suffering a strange dearth of astronomical objects: the **Great Rift**, in the thick of the **Milky Way**.

To the unaided eye, the Milky Way looks like a stream of milk spilt across the sky, but binoculars or a small telescope resolve the mistiness into millions of individual stars, the denizens of our home Galaxy, stacked up one behind the other as we gaze into its depths.

But even a glance at **Cygnus** reveals a dark gash in the Milky Way. William Herschel, the first astronomer to map the Galaxy, thought the Great Rift was a genuine void in the star distribution. But now we know that it's a murky swathe of sooty dust running through our Galaxy and blocking the light from the stars beyond.

SEPTEMBER'S TOPIC: SUBRAHMANYAN CHANDRASEKHAR

It would take weeks for the young Indian astrophysicist Subramanyan Chandrasekhar (1910–95), universally known as Chandra, to travel by boat and train from Bombay to Cambridge in 1930, so he set himself a solitary task to keep busy. It would lead him to a Nobel Prize, and a NASA orbiting observatory named after him.

Astronomers already knew that a star like the Sun ends its days as a white dwarf: a superdense object with roughly the Sun's mass, but no larger than a city.

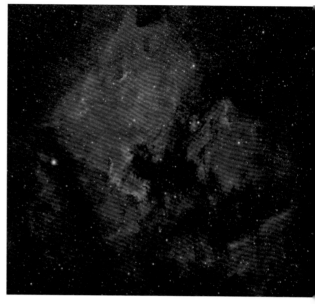

No telescope needed! Observing from Guernsey, Jean Dean obtained this wide-angle view with a Canon 85-mm EF lens attached to a Starlight Xpress 814 mono CCD fitted with LRGB filters, for a total integration time of 1 hour 50 minutes.

In the 1920s, they assumed this would be the fate of all stars, however massive.

During the long journey, Chandra applied Einstein's Theory of Relativity to the electrons whizzing around inside a white dwarf. He was staggered to find that the more massive a white dwarf, the less force the electrons could muster to support the star against its own gravity. Above a certain mass (1.4 solar masses, now called the Chandrasekhar limit), the white dwarf would collapse completely.

His colleagues at Cambridge initially disparaged the young scientist's seemingly nonsensical result. But Chandra was right. He had proved that the most massive stars end up as what we now call black holes.

OBSERVING TIP

It's best to view your favourite objects when they're well clear of the horizon. If you observe them low down, you're looking through a large thickness of the atmosphere – which is always shifting and turbulent. It's like trying to observe the outside world from the bottom of a swimming pool! This turbulence makes the stars appear to twinkle. Low-down planets also twinkle – although to a lesser extent, because they subtend tiny discs, and aren't so affected.

SEPTEMBER'S PICTURE

You'll find this distinctive pair of nebulae close to the star **Deneb**, in Cygnus (the Swan). The aptly named **North America Nebula** is ten times the size of the Full Moon, but so faint you'll need binoculars or small telescope to observe it. With a bit of imagination, you can work out why its companion is dubbed the **Pelican Nebula**.

Appearances are deceptive, though. These are not two separate nebulae, but a single immense cloud of glowing gas – 140 light years across – with a foreground belt of interstellar dust and gas blotting out its middle region. One edge of this dark cloud appears in silhouette as the 'Gulf of Mexico,' while the other side defines the shape of the Pelican's distended bill. It also obscures the intensely hot star lighting up the whole nebula: the Bajamar (Bahama) Star, named for its location off the 'eastern coast' of the North America Nebula.

SUNDAY	MONDAY	TUESDAY	WEDNESDAY	THURSDAY	FRIDAY	SATURDAY
					1	2
3	4 Moon near Jupiter	5 Moon near Pleiades	6 11:21 pm Last Quarter Moon	7	8	9
10 Moon near Castor and Pollux (am)	11 Moon near Venus (am)	12 Moon near Venus (am)	13 Moon near Regulus (am)	14	15 2:40 am New Moon	16
17	18 Venus at maximum brightness	19 Neptune opposition	20	21	22 8:32 pm First Quarter Moon; Mercury E elongation	23 Autumn Equinox
24	25	26 Moon near Saturn	27	28	29 10:57 am Full Moon	30

SPECIAL EVENTS

- **4 September:** Jupiter is right next to the Moon, with the Pleiades to the left (Chart 9a).
- **5 September:** look just above the Moon to spot the glimmering Pleiades – a gorgeous sight in binoculars – with Jupiter well to the right (Chart 9a).
- **11 September, before dawn:** a lovely sight, as the crescent Moon hangs above Venus.
- **12 September, before dawn:** Venus forms a gorgeous duo with the crescent Moon to its left (Chart 9b).
- **18 September:** Venus reaches its greatest brilliance as a Morning Star, at magnitude –4.5.
- **19 September:** visible throughout the night, Neptune is opposite to the Sun, and at its nearest to the Earth at 4324 million km (see Planet Watch).
- **23 September, 7.50 am:** nights become longer than days as the Sun moves south of the Equator at the Autumn Equinox.
- This month, NASA's OSIRIS-REx spacecraft is due to return to Earth, carrying samples of rock and dust from asteroid Bennu.

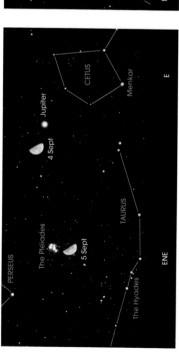

9a 4–5 September, 11 pm. The Moon cruises past Jupiter and the Pleiades.

9b 12 September, 5 am. The crescent Moon with Venus.

• In the southern skies, **Saturn** lies in Aquarius and is above the horizon all night long. The ringworld shines at magnitude +0.5, and the Moon lies nearby on 26 September.

• But it's the month to focus on its fainter neighbour in the sky: **Neptune**, in Pisces, is closest to the Earth on 19 September (see Special Events), and is visible throughout the night – though with the proviso you need binoculars or a telescope to see it all! Though Neptune is four times wider than the Earth, its distance means the planet glows at a feeble magnitude +7.8, less than half the brightness of the faintest star you can see with the naked eye. You'll need a moderate telescope to see Neptune as anything more than a point of light, but it's always a thrill to spot the outermost planet of the Sun's family.

• The giant of the Solar System, **Jupiter**, rises about 9 pm, at magnitude –2.7 in Aries. The Moon lies nearby on 4 September (Chart 9a).

• **Uranus** is also in Aries, near the border with Taurus. It's also rising around 9 pm, but at a pretty dismal magnitude +5.7.

• The Morning Star appears in all its glory this month, as **Venus** speeds upwards in the dawn sky. By the end of September, the planet is rising as 3 am, so early we see it against a truly dark sky, and at its maximum brightness (magnitude –4.5). There's a pretty sight when the crescent Moon hangs nearby on the mornings of 11 and 12 September (Chart 9b).

• From 20 September, **Mercury** (magnitude –0.5) rises around 5 am, well to the lower left of Venus. It's at maximum separation from the Sun on 22 September.

• **Mars** is too close to the Sun to be visible in September.

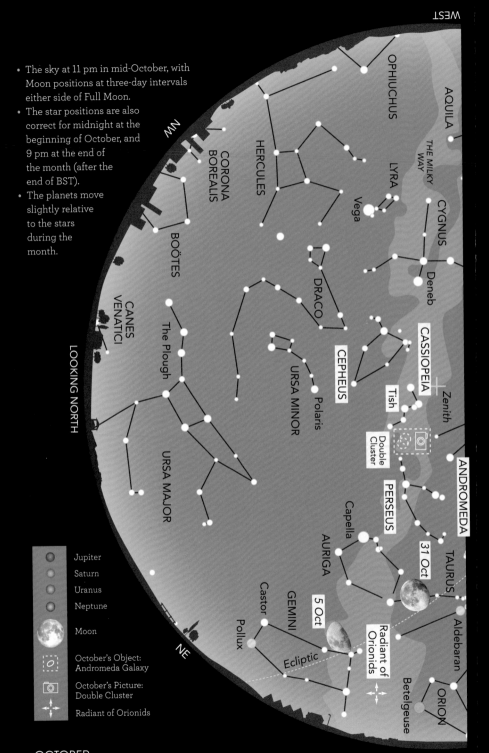

- The sky at 11 pm in mid-October, with Moon positions at three-day intervals either side of Full Moon.
- The star positions are also correct for midnight at the beginning of October, and 9 pm at the end of the month (after the end of BST).
- The planets move slightly relative to the stars during the month.

WEST

OPHIUCHUS

AQUILA

NW

CORONA BOREALIS

HERCULES

LYRA

THE MILKY WAY

CYGNUS

Vega

Deneb

BOÖTES

DRACO

CEPHEUS

CASSIOPEIA

Zenith

CANES VENATICI

The Plough

URSA MINOR

Polaris

Tish

Double Cluster

ANDROMEDA

LOOKING NORTH

URSA MAJOR

PERSEUS

Capella

31 Oct

TAURUS

AURIGA

Castor

GEMINI

5 Oct

Radiant of Orionids

Aldebaran

NE

Pollux

Ecliptic

Betelgeuse

ORION

Jupiter
Saturn
Uranus
Neptune

Moon

October's Object:
Andromeda Galaxy

October's Picture:
Double Cluster

Radiant of Orionids

OCTOBER

EAST

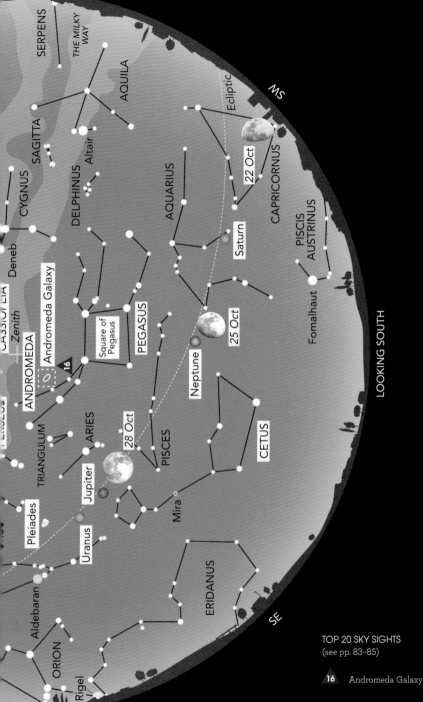

SERPENS

THE MILKY WAY

AQUILA

SAGITTA

CYGNUS

DELPHINUS

Altair

Deneb

CASSIOPEIA

Zenith

ANDROMEDA

Andromeda Galaxy

16

0

Square of Pegasus

PEGASUS

PERSEUS

TRIANGULUM

ARIES

Pleiades

Jupiter

Uranus

Aldebaran

ORION

Rigel

Ecliptic

MS

22 Oct

CAPRICORNUS

AQUARIUS

Saturn

PISCIS AUSTRINUS

Fomalhaut

Neptune

25 Oct

28 Oct

PISCES

CETUS

Mira

ERIDANUS

SE

LOOKING SOUTH

OCTOBER

TOP 20 SKY SIGHTS
(see pp. 83–85)

16   Andromeda Galaxy

October's sky is pretty devoid of showy constellations. In the southern sky, neither the **Square of Pegasus** nor **Andromeda** attached to its side are guaranteed to thrill. But look to the east, where the brilliant lights of winter are starting to appear, spearheaded by the beautiful star cluster of the **Pleiades**. Watch out for pieces of Halley's Comet smashing into our atmosphere on 21 October, and a minor lunar eclipse on 28 October.

OCTOBER'S CONSTELLATION

Look almost overhead for five stars in a distinctive W-shape. To the Greeks, this constellation represented Queen **Cassiopeia** of Ethiopia, who ruled with her husband King **Cepheus**. The hero **Perseus** rescued their daughter **Andromeda** from a ravaging sea monster (**Cetus**), and these characters are now all immortalised in the heavens.

Unusually, the central star in Cassiopeia is known by its Chinese name – **Tsih** (the Whip). This unstable star – 55,000 times brighter than the Sun – is spinning around at breakneck pace, flinging out streams of gas.

OBSERVING TIP

The Andromeda Galaxy is often described as the furthest object 'easily visible to the unaided eye'. It can be a bit elusive, though – especially if you are suffering from light pollution. The trick is to memorise Andromeda's pattern of stars, and then to look slightly to the side of where you expect the galaxy to be. This technique – called 'averted vision' – causes the image to fall on the outer region of your retina, which is more sensitive to light than the central region that's evolved to discern fine details. The technique is also crucial when you want to observe the faintest nebulae or galaxies through a telescope.

Cassiopeia has hosted several supernovae, including an exploding star seen by Danish astronomer Tycho Brahe in 1572. The fireball from a later supernova is now the most prominent radio source in the sky, Cassiopeia A.

OCTOBER'S OBJECT

Take advantage of autumn's dark nights to pick out the Milky Way's near twin, the **Andromeda Galaxy** (catalogued as M31 in Charles Messier's list of fuzzy patches). Visible to the unaided eye, the Andromeda Galaxy covers an area four times the size of the Full Moon. Like our Milky Way, it's a spiral galaxy, but you won't see much sign of that – even through a telescope – because Andromeda is almost edge-on to us.

The Andromeda Galaxy lies 2.5 million light years away, and it's a little larger than the Milky Way. Like our own Galaxy, Andromeda has two bright companion galaxies as well as a flotilla of orbiting dwarf galaxies.

While other galaxies are receding from us in the expanding Universe, Andromeda is unusual in approaching the Milky Way. The two galaxies will merge in about four billion years' time. The pile-up will create a giant elliptical galaxy – nicknamed 'Milkomeda' – devoid of gas and dominated by ancient red giant stars.

OCTOBER'S TOPIC: SPOTTY PLANETS

Mighty **Jupiter** dominates the night sky, and even a small telescope reveals its most famous feature. The Great Red Spot is a storm that's bigger than planet Earth, and powered by winds raging at over 430 kilometres per hour. Its red colour is due to sunburn, where the storm's high clouds are being blasted by the Sun's ultraviolet light. Over the past century, the Great Red Spot has been shrinking, but there's no sign yet of it disappearing.

Jupiter isn't alone in being a spotty world: all four outer planets can break out in a temporary rash. In 1933, **Saturn** sported a huge white spot: it was discovered by the comedian Will Hay, who was also an amateur astronomer. Saturn's storms recur every 20 years or so.

When the spaceprobe Voyager 2 swept past **Uranus** in 1986 it found a featureless world. But astronomers on Earth saw a dark spot appear on Uranus in 2006, and white spots erupted in 2014.

The outermost planet, **Neptune**, put on a splendid show for Voyager 2's cameras in 1989. Much more active than Uranus,

Ralph Smith imaged the Double Cluster from Lisburn, County Antrim, with a Sky-Watcher Evostar 72ED DS-PRO refractor telescope fitted with a field flattener, and ZWO 2600MC colour camera cooled to –10°C. The total exposure time was 1 hour 27 minutes.

with winds up to 2200 kilometres per hour – the fastest in the Solar System – Neptune sported a giant dark spot and speeding white clouds.

OCTOBER'S PICTURE

The **Double Cluster** in Perseus is a glorious sight in binoculars. Medium-sized telescopes reveal hundreds of stars in each cluster, with splendid colour contrasts – as you can see in Ralph Smith's vibrant image. The brightest stars are either blue-white supergiants, still burning hydrogen, or red supergiants in the last phase of their lives.

Some 7500 light years away, the Double Cluster is only 14 million years old. Our Sun, by comparison, has been around for almost 5 *billion* years.

SUNDAY	MONDAY	TUESDAY	WEDNESDAY	THURSDAY	FRIDAY	SATURDAY
1 Moon near Jupiter	**2** Moon between Jupiter and Pleiades	**3** Moon near Aldebaran and the Pleiades	**4**	**5**	**6** 2:48 pm Last Quarter Moon near Castor and Pollux	**7**
8	**9**	**10** Moon near Venus and Regulus (am)	**11** Moon near Venus and Regulus (am)	**12**	**13**	**14** 6.55 pm New Moon: annular solar eclipse
15	**16**	**17**	**18** Moon near Antares	**19**	**20**	**21** Orionids
22 4.29 am First Quarter Moon; Orionids (am)	**23** Venus W elongation; Moon near Saturn	**24** Moon near Saturn	**25**	**26**	**27**	**28** 9.24 pm Full Moon near Jupiter, partial lunar eclipse: supermoon
29 BST ends; Moon between Jupiter and Pleiades	**30** Moon near the Pleiades	**31**				

⭐ SPECIAL EVENTS

- **1 October:** the Moon glides just above giant planet Jupiter.
- **2 October:** the Pleiades lie to the left of the Moon, with Jupiter to the right.
- **3 October:** the Moon passes between Aldebaran and the Pleiades.
- **10 October, before dawn:** the crescent Moon hangs above Venus, with Regulus in between (Chart 10a).
- **11 October, before dawn:** Venus and the crescent Moon make another stunning pairing, with Regulus above.
- **14 October:** an annular eclipse of the Sun is visible from the western United States, central America, Colombia and Brazil. It's partial as seen from the rest of the Americas, but nothing is visible from Europe.
- **Night of 21/22 October:** it's a great year for observing the **Orionid meteor shower,** debris from Halley's Comet smashing into Earth's atmosphere, after the Moon sets around 10 pm.
- **28 October:** there's a partial lunar eclipse, near to Jupiter, though only 12% of the Moon's silver face is obscured (Chart 10b). The eclipse is visible from Europe, Africa and Asia. It begins at 8.35 pm and ends at 9.53 pm.
- **29 October, 2 am:** the end of British Summer Time.
- **29 October:** the Moon hangs between Jupiter (right) and the Pleiades (left).
- **30 October:** the misty patch above the Moon is the Pleiades.

10a 10 October, 4 am. The Moon next to Venus and Regulus.

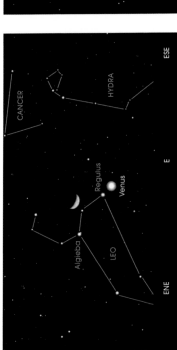

10b 28 October, 9.15 pm. Maximum of the lunar eclipse.

- **Jupiter** is brilliant in the south, lying in Aries and rising about 7 pm. At magnitude −2.9, the giant planet is far brighter than anything else in the evening sky, bar the Moon. On 1 October, these two major night-lights get together, with the Moon sailing over Jupiter. They meet again on 28 October, when the Full Moon is eclipsed.

- Well to the right of Jupiter, **Saturn** lies in Aquarius, at magnitude +0.6. The ringed planet sets around 2.30 am. The Moon is nearby on 23 and 24 October.

- Between these two massive planets lies distant **Neptune**, in Pisces. It skulks at magnitude +7.8, and sets about 5 am.

- **Uranus** (magnitude +5.6) is in Aries, rising around 7 pm.

Jupiter has been approaching Uranus for months, and the gap has narrowed to 8° by the start of October, but the giant planet then starts to back away again.

- Rising about 3 am, **Venus** appears as the dazzling Morning Star, at magnitude −4.4, reaching its greatest separation from the Sun on 23 October. It's joined by the crescent Moon, along with

Regulus, on the mornings of 10 and 11 October (see Special Events and Chart 10a).

- For the first few mornings of October, you may catch **Mercury** very low in the dawn twilight, at magnitude −1.0 and rising just before 6 am. But it then drops down into the pre-dawn glow and disappears from sight.

- **Mars** is lost in the Sun's glare all month.

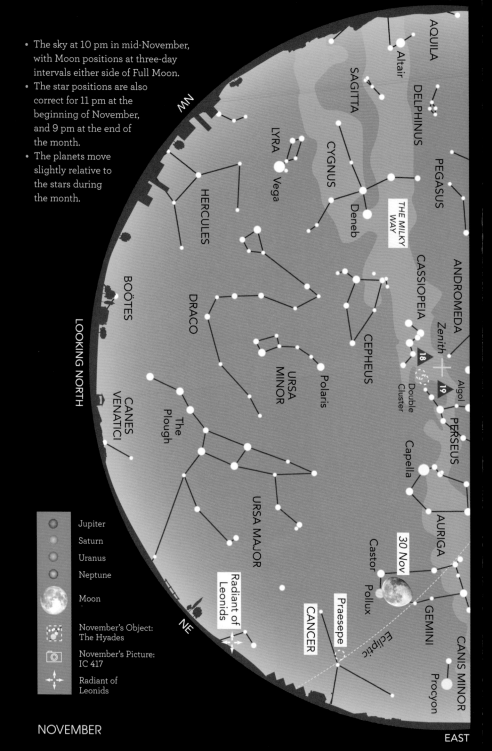

- The sky at 10 pm in mid-November, with Moon positions at three-day intervals either side of Full Moon.
- The star positions are also correct for 11 pm at the beginning of November, and 9 pm at the end of the month.
- The planets move slightly relative to the stars during the month.

WEST

NW

LOOKING NORTH

AQUILA

Altair

DELPHINUS

SAGITTA

PEGASUS

LYRA

Vega

CYGNUS

Deneb

THE MILKY WAY

CASSIOPEIA

ANDROMEDA

Zenith

HERCULES

18

Algol

BOÖTES

DRACO

CEPHEUS

Double Cluster

19

PERSEUS

URSA MINOR

Polaris

CANES VENATICI

The Plough

Capella

URSA MAJOR

AURIGA

Jupiter

Saturn

Uranus

Neptune

Moon

November's Object: The Hyades

November's Picture: IC 417

Radiant of Leonids

30 Nov

Castor

Pollux

GEMINI

Radiant of Leonids

CANCER

Praesepe

Ecliptic

CANIS MINOR

Procyon

NE

NOVEMBER

EAST

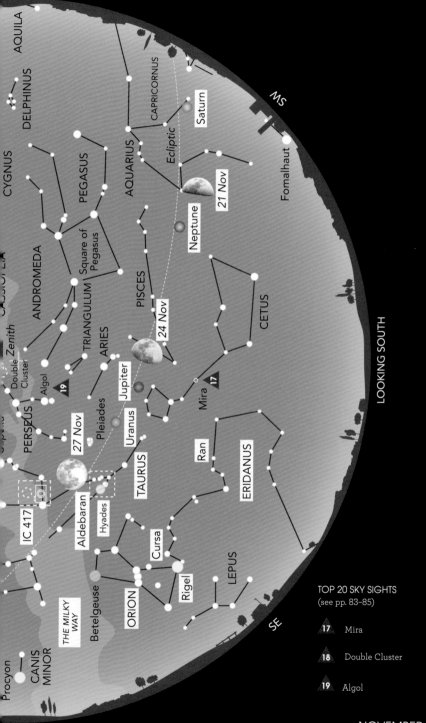

WEST

AQUILA

DELPHINUS

CYGNUS

CAPRICORNUS

Saturn

MS

Ecliptic

AQUARIUS

PEGASUS

21 Nov

Neptune

Fomalhaut

Square of
Pegasus

ANDROMEDA

PISCES

Double *Zenith*
Cluster

TRIANGULUM

24 Nov

CETUS

ARIES

Algol

PERSEUS

Jupiter

Mira

17

19

27 Nov

Pleiades

Uranus

Ran

IC 417

Aldebaran

Hyades

TAURUS

ERIDANUS

*THE MILKY
WAY*

Cursa

LEPUS

Betelgeuse

ORION

Rigel

Procyon

CANIS
MINOR

LOOKING SOUTH

SE

EAST

NOVEMBER

TOP 20 SKY SIGHTS
(see pp. 83–85)

17   Mira

18   Double Cluster

19   Algol

Brilliant **Jupiter** steals the show, at its closest to the Earth as the month opens. There's more subtle beauty in the **Milky Way**, which rears overhead on these dark November nights and provides a stunning inside perspective on the huge Galaxy that is our home in space. Sweep along it with binoculars, and you'll see that this glowing ribbon of stars is studded with star clusters and nebulae.

NOVEMBER'S CONSTELLATION

A long, winding constellation, the celestial river **Eridanus** rises in the star **Cursa** (the Footstool) just above brilliant **Rigel** in **Orion**, and flows downwards over 70° of the sky, making it the sixth-largest star pattern. Eridanus is probably named after the ancient city of Eridu, at the mouth of the River Euphrates.

Ran (Epsilon Eridani) is one of the closest Sun-like stars, just 10.5 light years away: it's surrounded by two dusty discs and a planet slightly less massive than Jupiter.

Below the horizon on the Star Chart lies Acamar, the river's original mouth. It was the southernmost star in Eridanus visible to ancient astronomers, and small telescopes reveal it's actually a close pair of white stars. When European explorers travelled southwards in the Age of Discovery, they found a brighter star below Acamar; astronomers named it Achernar, and extended the river to terminate in this first magnitude star.

NOVEMBER'S OBJECT

According to Greek legend, the V-shaped **Hyades** star cluster, forming the 'head' of **Taurus** (the Bull), was a group of nymphs who cared for the wine-god Bacchus as a baby. To the Romans, these stars were little pigs, while the Chinese saw a net full of rabbits.

The Hyades is the nearest star cluster to the Earth, lying 153 light years away. With the unaided eye, you can make out about 15 stars in this group, while a large telescope reveals a population of several hundred fainter stars. (Although **Aldebaran** looks as though it's in the Hyades, this red giant lies at only half the distance.)

With an age of 625 million years the Hyades is quite young on the cosmic scale. And it has a twin: **Praesepe** – the Beehive Cluster in **Cancer** – is the same age and moves in the same direction, so the two were most likely born together.

NOVEMBER'S TOPIC:
THE MULTIVERSE

We live in an absolutely vast Universe. Our most powerful telescopes reveal galaxies out to 13 billion light years away – the maximum distance light has been able to travel since the Big Bang. The Universe beyond could be infinite. Even so, some cosmologists want more . . .

Our Universe probably began as a tiny random blip in a pre-existing vacuum; it got out of control and blew up into the Big Bang that created everything we know. In this case, we'd expect that other primordial blips would have spawned other universes, too, in different dimensions.

This whole collection of universes – including our own – is generally called the

Multiverse. Each of these universes would have different laws of Nature, and in most of them matter and forces like gravity would be unstable. Only a very select few, including our own Universe, have laws of Nature that permit atoms to be stable, and planets to follow regular orbit around their stars – hence allowing life to evolve.

NOVEMBER'S PICTURE

Sometimes called the Spider Nebula, **IC 417** looks distinctly one-legged in this colourful shot by Sara Wager; wide-angle images reveal other appendages attached to the bright 'body' at the right.

Situated in **Auriga** at a distance of 6700 light years, IC 417 is a glowing

Observing under dark Spanish skies, Sara Wager aimed her 235-mm f/10 Celestron C9.25 telescope (with Celestron 0.63 reducer) at IC 417, and imaged it using an Atik 460EXM camera. She took 32 exposures through an H-alpha filter and 31 through an OIII filter, each of 30 minutes, giving a total exposure time of 31.5 hours.

OBSERVING TIP

With Christmas on the way, you may be thinking of buying a telescope as a present for a budding stargazer. Beware! Unscrupulous websites and mail-order catalogues often advertise small telescopes that boast huge magnifications, but all they do is show you a large blurry image. To see planets and stars sharply, you need to use a magnification no more than twice the diameter of the lens or mirror in millimetres. So if you see an advertisement for a 75-mm telescope, beware of any claims for a magnification greater than 150 times.

nebula that's heated by young stars born just a few million years ago.

The unusual streamer to the left looks as though it's been squirted out of the main nebula. But appearances are deceptive. It's actually the glowing rim of a dark cloud, illuminated by a hot star to the north (off the top of this image).

SUNDAY	MONDAY	TUESDAY	WEDNESDAY	THURSDAY	FRIDAY	SATURDAY
			1 Jupiter closest to Earth	2	3 Jupiter opposition; Moon near Castor and Pollux	4
5 8.37 am Last Quarter Moon	6	7 Moon near Regulus (am)	8	9 Moon very near Venus (am), day-time occultation	10	11 Moon near Spica (am)
12	13 9.27 am New Moon; Uranus opposition	14	15	16	17 Leonid meteor shower	18 Leonid meteor shower (am)
19	20 10.50 am First Quarter Moon; near Saturn	21	22 Venus near Spica (am)	23	24	25 Moon near Jupiter
26 Moon near Pleiades	27 9.16 am Full Moon	28	29 Venus near Spica (am)	30 Venus near Spica (am); Moon near Castor and Pollux		

SPECIAL EVENTS

- **1 November:** Jupiter is closest to the Earth, 596 million km away (see Planet Watch).
- **3 November:** two days after its closest approach, Jupiter lies opposite to the Sun in the sky.
- **9 November, before dawn:** there's a dazzling duo in the morning twilight, as the crescent Moon pairs up with glorious Venus (Chart 11a). Follow Venus with a telescope as the day dawns (being very careful not to swing it towards the Sun), and you'll see the Moon move right in front of the Morning Star between roughly 9.45 and 10.45 am (Chart 11b).
- **13 November:** Uranus is at its closest to the Earth – 2787 million km away – and opposite to the Sun in the sky (see Planet Watch).
- **Night of 17/18 November:** maximum of the annual **Leonid meteor shower**. It's a great year for observing these fragments of Comet Tempel-Tuttle impacting our atmosphere as shooting stars. Occasionally in the past, we've been treated to a storm of Leonid meteors. The rate has been low for many years, but this year the number is expected to perk up, with the chance of some bright fireballs.
- **20 November:** Saturn lies just above the First Quarter Moon.
- **25 November:** the bright 'star' near the Moon is giant planet Jupiter.
- **26 November:** the Moon passes under the Pleiades.

11b *9 November, 9.46 am. Venus disappears behind the Moon.*

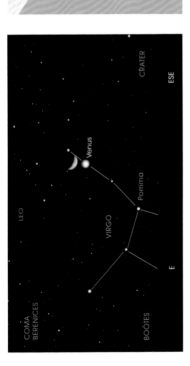

11a *9 November, 4 am. The crescent Moon heads towards Venus.*

- Giant planet **Jupiter** is closest to the Earth on 1 November (see Special Events), and two days later it's at opposition – in line with the Sun and the Earth. As a result, Jupiter is at its brightest this month, at a magnificent magnitude –2.9. The megaworld lies in Aries, and is visible all night long. The Moon passes nearby on 25 November. With binoculars you can spot Jupiter's four biggest moons, shifting in position night by night; while a small telescope reveals its roiling clouds and the monster storm that's dubbed the Great Red Spot.

- **Uranus** is also in Aries, lying between Jupiter and the Pleiades. The seventh planet is closest to the Earth and at opposition on 13 November (see Special Events). At magnitude +5.6, Uranus is just visible to the unaided eye, if you know exactly where to look. Through binoculars, it resembles a slightly greenish star. You'll need a moderate-power telescope to discern its disc and the largest moons.

- You'll find **Saturn** swimming among the faint stars of Aquarius. At magnitude +0.8, the ringworld sets about 11.30 pm. The First Quarter Moon is just below on 20 November.

- **Neptune** (magnitude +7.8) lies on the border of Aquarius and Pisces, and sets around 2 am.

- Brilliant **Venus** rises around 3 am, resplendent at magnitude –4.3. The crescent Moon is extremely close before dawn on 9 November and occults Venus later that morning (see Special Events, plus Charts 11a and 11b). Venus passes above Spica on the mornings of 29 and 30 November.

- **Mercury** and **Mars** are too close to the Sun to be visible in November.

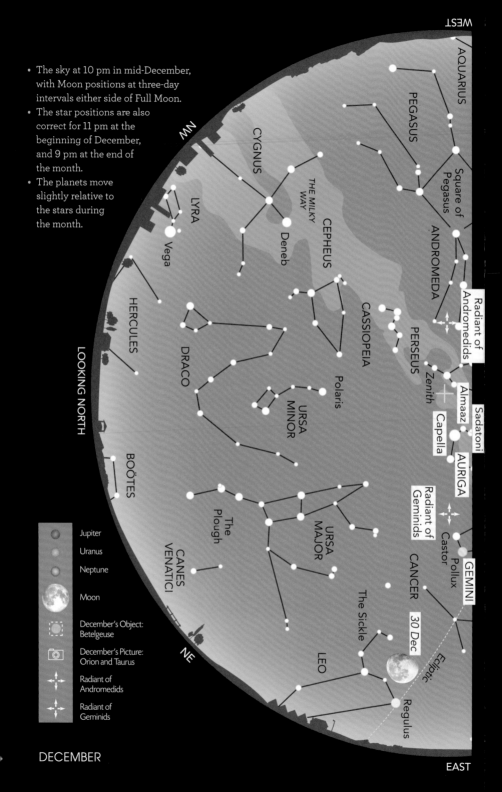

- The sky at 10 pm in mid-December, with Moon positions at three-day intervals either side of Full Moon.
- The star positions are also correct for 11 pm at the beginning of December, and 9 pm at the end of the month.
- The planets move slightly relative to the stars during the month.

LOOKING NORTH

DECEMBER

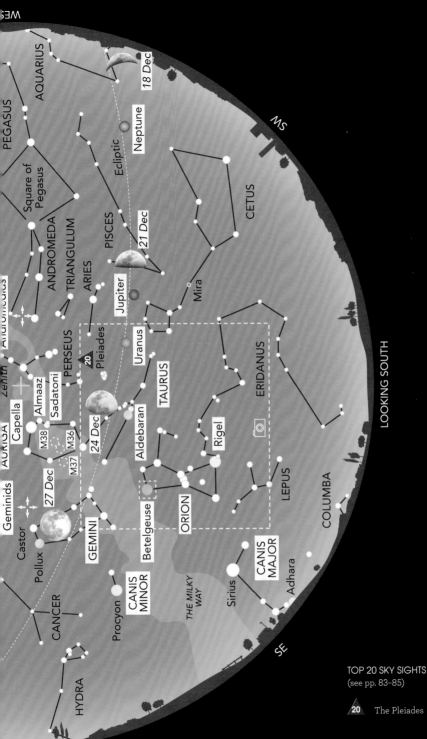

WEST

PEGASUS

AQUARIUS

18 Dec

Square of
Pegasus

ANDROMEDA

TRIANGULUM

Ecliptic

Neptune

PISCES

ARIES

21 Dec

Jupiter

Mira

CETUS

Zenith

PERSEUS

Pleiades

Uranus

20

AURIGA

Capella

Almaaz

Sadatoni

M38

M36

M37

24 Dec

Aldebaran

TAURUS

ERIDANUS

Geminids

27 Dec

Rigel

Castor

GEMINI

Betelgeuse

ORION

LEPUS

Pollux

COLUMBA

CANCER

Procyon

CANIS
MINOR

THE MILKY
WAY

CANIS
MAJOR

Sirius

Adhara

HYDRA

NW

SW

LOOKING SOUTH

SE

TOP 20 SKY SIGHTS
(see pp. 83–85)

20   The Pleiades

DECEMBER

Brave the winter chill to enjoy the celestial pyrotechnics of the regular **Geminid meteor shower**, and possibly a brilliant display of the rarely seen **Andromedid meteors**. On the stellar front, **Orion**, with his hunting dogs **Canis Major** and **Canis Minor**, is fighting **Taurus** (the Bull). Spectating are the hero twins of **Gemini** and the charioteer **Auriga**. Meanwhile, faint **Lepus**, the timid Hare, cowers at Orion's feet.

DECEMBER'S CONSTELLATION

Sparkling overhead, **Auriga** (the Charioteer) is named after the Greek hero Erichthonius, who invented the four-horse chariot. The ancient Babylonians, on the other hand, saw Auriga as a shepherd's crook.

Capella, the sixth-brightest star in the sky, means 'the Little Nanny Goat'. It consists of two stars, each 75 times brighter than the Sun, orbiting more closely than the Earth circles the Sun.

Nearby, you'll find two eclipsing binaries: stars that change in brightness because a companion passes in front. **Sadatoni** is an orange star eclipsed every 972 days by a blue partner. **Almaaz** has a companion star that's completely hidden inside a huge swirling disc of black cosmic dust. Every 27 years, this dark disc moves in front of Almaaz and eclipses it for two years.

And bring out your binoculars (better still, a small telescope) to view three very pretty star clusters within the outline of Auriga, **M36**, **M37** and **M38**.

DECEMBER'S OBJECT

Betelgeuse is perhaps the most famous star in the sky. It's a big star in every way – 750 times wider than our Sun, and 100,000 times brighter. If placed in our Solar System, Betelgeuse would extend well beyond the orbit of Mars.

Nearing the end of its life, Betelgeuse is running out of nuclear fuel. Its brightness changes as the star's loosely held outer layers wobble about. In 2020, the star dimmed seriously as it ejected an obscuring cloud of dark dust. Before long on the cosmic timescale – within the next 100,000 years perhaps – Betelgeuse will explode as a supernova.

The greatest debate about Betelgeuse is not about its size or its fate – but how to pronounce its name! Since the 1988 film *Beetlejuice*, that's how almost everyone says it. But scholars beg to differ. The Arabs named the star *Yad al-Jauzā'*, meaning 'the hand of the central one [Orion]', but later the initial 'Y' was transliterated as a 'B'. To be correct, then, pronounce it 'Yad-al-jow-za' – but don't blame me if all you get are blank looks!

OBSERVING TIP

Hold a 'meteor party' to check out the year's best celestial firework show, the Geminid meteor shower on 13/14 December. You don't need any optical equipment: the ideal viewing equipment is your unaided eye, plus a warm sleeping bag and a lounger. Everyone should look in different directions, so you can cover the whole sky. Shout out 'Meteor!' when you see a shooting star. One of your party can record the observations, using a watch, notepad and red torch.

DECEMBER'S TOPIC: HALLEY'S COMET

In 1986, it was hailed as a 'once in a lifetime event': Halley's Comet would swing close to the Sun and be visible to the unaided eye from planet Earth. This month, the celestial wayfarer reaches its furthest point from the Sun, and begins to freefall back into the inner Solar System for its next apparition, in 2061.

For many, Halley's return in 1986 was disappointing. The comet and the Earth were on opposite sides of the Sun, so in our skies it was the faintest apparition in 2000 years. From the northern hemisphere, it wasn't visible at all from light polluted cities. Even viewed from south of the equator, views of the magnitude +2.1 comet were far from spectacular.

We were treated, though, to the first detailed views of a comet's nucleus, when the European Giotto probe risked the high-speed dust particles in the comet's head to snap the nucleus in close-up. It revealed a dark, potato-shaped lump of dirty ice ejecting jets of steam.

For us on Earth, next time will be better. In July 2061, Halley's Comet will be ten times brighter, at magnitude −0.3, and visible from the northern hemisphere as well as the south. Well worth waiting half a lifetime!

Just outside the village of Wilton, Wiltshire, Jo Bourne framed this lovely view in her Sony A7 III camera with a Sony FE 20-mm f/1.8 G lens, and a lens heater to avoid dewing up. A light-pollution filter cut out background glow, while a Starglow filter enhanced the brighter stars in the constellations. An intervalometer automatically shot 15 × 30-second exposures at ISO 3200. She stacked the images in Sequator and edited in Lightroom.

DECEMBER'S PICTURE

There's nothing more inspiring than stepping outside on a frosty night and taking in the celestial tableau of the brilliant sparkling winter constellations, vividly captured here by Jo Bourne.

Centre stage is the great hunter, **Orion**, with his belt hitched to a jaunty angle and two jewels in his tunic – ruby Betelgeuse at one shoulder and sapphire **Rigel** on his lower hem. Facing him to the upper right is the mighty bull, **Taurus**, with blood-red **Aldebaran** marking his angry eye.

SUNDAY	MONDAY	TUESDAY	WEDNESDAY	THURSDAY	FRIDAY	SATURDAY
					1	**2** Andromedids
31 Moon near Regulus						
3 Andromedids (am); Moon near Regulus	**4** Mercury E elongation	**5** 5.49 am Last Quarter Moon	**6**	**7**	**8** Moon near Spica (am)	**9** Moon near Venus (am)
10 Moon below Venus (am)	**11**	**12** 11.32 pm New Moon	**13** Geminids	**14** Geminids (am)	**15**	**16**
17 Moon near Saturn	**18**	**19** 6.39 pm First Quarter Moon	**20**	**21**	**22** Winter Solstice; Moon near Jupiter	**23**
24 Moon between Aldebaran and Pleiades	**25**	**26**	**27** 0.33 am Full Moon	**28** Moon near Castor and Pollux	**29**	**30** Moon near Regulus

SPECIAL EVENTS

- **Night of 2/3 December:** we may be treated to a rare display of the **Andromedids**, meteors from the defunct Biela's Comet, which broke up in 1846. Tonight the Earth smashes into debris that it shed in 1649. You may see a shooting star every minute.
- **8 December, before dawn:** the crescent Moon lies above Spica, with Venus down to the lower left.
- **9 December, before dawn:** Venus and the crescent Moon make a splendid pair in the south-eastern sky, with Spica to the upper right (Chart 12a).
- **9 December:** Halley's Comet at its furthest distance from the Sun, 5257 million km (see Topic).

- **10 December, before dawn:** you'll find the thinnest crescent Moon down below Venus.
- **Night of 13/14 December:** look out for the best annual show of celestial fireworks, unspoilt by moonlight. The bright slow shooting stars of the **Geminid meteor shower**, are – unusually – debris not from a comet, but from an asteroid, called Phaethon.

- **17 December:** Saturn lies above the Moon.
- **22 December, 03.27 am:** the Winter Solstice, when the Sun reaches its southernmost point, giving the northern hemisphere the shortest day and the longest night.
- **22 December:** the brilliant 'star' near the Moon is giant planet Jupiter (Chart 12b).

12a 9 December, 6 am. The crescent Moon with Venus and Spica.

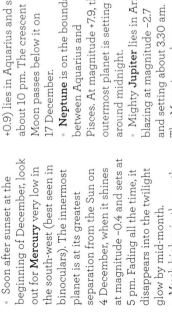

12b 22 December, 10 pm. The Moon pairs up with Jupiter.

- Soon after sunset at the beginning of December, look out for **Mercury** very low in the south-west (best seen in binoculars). The innermost planet is at its greatest separation from the Sun on 4 December, when it shines at magnitude −0.4 and sets at 5 pm. Fading all the time, it disappears into the twilight glow by mid-month.
- Much higher in the south-west, **Saturn** (magnitude +0.9) lies in Aquarius and sets about 10 pm. The crescent Moon passes below it on 17 December.
- **Neptune** is on the boundary between Aquarius and Pisces. At magnitude +7.9, the outermost planet is setting around midnight.
- Mighty **Jupiter** lies in Aries, blazing at magnitude −2.7 and setting about 3.30 am. The Moon is nearby on 22 December (Chart 12b).

- Also in Aries, **Uranus** (magnitude +5.6) sinks below the horizon around 5 am.
- If you're up really late – or getting up early – you'll find **Venus** rising in the south-east around 4 am. The Morning Star is brilliant at magnitude −4.1, and through a telescope you can see its globe more than half-illuminated. The crescent Moon makes a lovely pair with Venus on the morning of 9 December (see Special Events and Chart 12a).
- **Mars** is lost in the Sun's glare this month.

Can you see the planets? It's a common question; and the answer is a resounding 'yes!' Some of our cosmic neighbours are the brightest objects in the night sky after the Moon. As they're so close, you can watch them getting up to their antics from night to night. And planetary debris – leftovers from the birth of the Solar System – can light up our skies as glowing comets and the celestial fireworks of a meteor shower.

THE SUN-HUGGERS

Mercury and Venus orbit the Sun more closely than our own planet, so they never seem to stray far from our local star: you can spot them in the west after sunset, or the east before dawn, but never all night long. At *elongation*, the planet is at its greatest separation from the Sun, though – as you can see in the diagram (right) – that's not when the planet is at its brightest. Through a telescope, Mercury and Venus (technically known as the *inferior planets*) show phases like the Moon – from a thin crescent to a full globe – as they orbit the Sun.

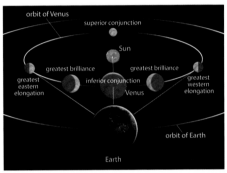

Venus (and Mercury) show phases like the Moon as they orbit the Sun.

Mercury

In the evening sky, Mercury makes its best appearance in April, is visible low down in July, and then puts on another brave show in December. The innermost planet has good morning apparitions in January–February and September–October (it's lost in the dawn light even at maximum elongation in May).

Venus

For the first seven months of 2023, Venus appears as the Evening Star. Then, in August, it swings by the Sun and re-emerges as the Morning Star for the rest of the year.

Maximum elongations of Mercury in 2023	
Date	Separation
30 January	25° west
11 April	20° east
29 May	25° west
10 August	27° east
22 September	18° west
4 December	21° east

Maximum elongations of Venus in 2023	
Date	Separation
4 June	45° east
23 October	46° west

WORLDS BEYOND

A planet orbiting the Sun beyond the Earth (known in the jargon as a *superior planet*) is visible at all times of night, as we look outwards into the Solar System.

It lies due south at midnight when the Sun, the Earth and the planet are all in line – a time known as *opposition* (see the diagram, right). Around this time the Earth lies nearest to the planet, although the date of closest approach (and the planet's maximum brightness) may differ by a few days because the planets' orbits are not circular.

Mars

After its brilliant opposition in December 2022, the Red Planet fades rapidly as the Earth pulls away, though it remains visible in the evening sky right through to the end of July After that, Mars is lost in the Sun's glow for the rest of the year.

● Where to find Mars	
January–March	Taurus
April–early May	Gemini
Late May–mid-June	Cancer
Late June –July	Leo

Jupiter

The giant planet is brilliant in the evening sky until the end of March, lying in Pisces. Jupiter reappears before dawn in mid-May, moving into Aries where it remains for the rest of the year. The planet is closest to the Earth on **1 November**, and reaches opposition on **3 November**.

Saturn

In January you can catch the ringed planet in Capricornus after sunset. It then disappears behind the sun and reappears in the morning sky in April. By then, Saturn has shifted into Aquarius and it stays in this constellation until the end of 2023. On **27 August**, Saturn is at opposition and at its closest to the Earth.

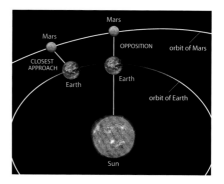

Mars (and the outer planets) line up with the Sun and Earth at opposition, but they are brightest at their point of closest approach.

Uranus

Up until April, the seventh planet is visible in the evening sky: from parts of Britain and Ireland, there's a rare chance to see the Moon occult Uranus on **1 January**. The planet emerges from the Sun's glow in the morning sky at the end of June, and reaches opposition on **13 November**. Uranus lies in Aries all year.

Neptune

The most distant planet lies on the border of Aquarius and Pisces throughout the year, and is at opposition on **19 September**. Neptune can be seen (though only through binoculars or a telescope) in January and February and then from May until the end of the year.

SOLAR ECLIPSES

On **20 April**, parts of Western Australia and Indonesia are treated to a hybrid solar eclipse: it starts as an annular eclipse, but over East Timor the eclipse becomes total, before it reverts to annular again. A partial eclipse is visible from Australia, Indonesia and the Philippines.

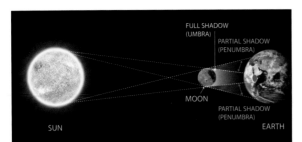

Where the dark central part (the umbra) of the Moon's shadow reaches the Earth, we are treated to a total solar eclipse. If the shadow doesn't quite reach the ground, we see an annular eclipse. People located within the penumbra observe a partial eclipse.

On **14 October**, people in the western United States, central America, Colombia and Brazil will experience an annular eclipse of the Sun. Maximum eclipse, with 95 per cent of the Sun obscured, occurs over Nicaragua. A partial eclipse is visible from all the Americas.

LUNAR ECLIPSES

On **28 October**, there's a partial eclipse of the Moon (not far from Jupiter) though only 12 per cent of the lunar surface is obscured. The eclipse is visible from Europe, Africa and Asia.

METEOR SHOWERS

Shooting stars, or *meteors*, are tiny specks of interplanetary dust burning up in the Earth's atmosphere. At certain times of year, Earth passes through a stream of debris (usually left by a comet) and we see a *meteor shower*. The meteors appear to emanate from a point in the sky known as the *radiant*. Most showers are known by the constellation in which the radiant lies.

It's fun and rewarding to hold a meteor party. Note the location, cloud cover, the time and brightness of each meteor and its direction through the stars – along with any persistent afterglow (train).

Table of annual meteor showers	
Meteor shower	Date of maximum
Quadrantids	3/4 January
Lyrids	22/23 April
Eta Aquarids	7 May (am)
Perseids	12/13 August
Orionids	21/22 October
Leonids	17/18 November
Geminids	13/14 December

COMETS

Comets are dirty snowballs from the outer Solar System. If they fall towards the Sun, its heat evaporates their ices to produce a gaseous head (*coma*) and sometimes dramatic tails. Although some comets are visible to the naked eye, use binoculars to reveal stunning details in the coma and the tail.

Hundreds of comets move round the Sun in small orbits. But many more don't return for thousands or even millions of years. Most comets are now discovered in professional surveys of the sky, but a few are still found by dedicated amateur astronomers. No bright comets are expected in 2023 at the time of writing, but watch out in case a brilliant new comet puts in a surprise appearance!

Here are some of the most popular sights in the night sky, in a season-by-season summary. It doesn't matter if you're a complete beginner, finding your way around the heavens with the unaided eye 👁 or binoculars 🔭; or if you're a seasoned stargazer, with a moderate telescope ⊁. There's something here for everyone.

Each sky sight comes with a brief description, and a guide as to how you can best see it. Many of the most delectable objects are faint, so avoid moonlight when you go out spotting. Most of all, enjoy!

SPRING

Praesepe   👁 🔭 ⊁

Constellation: Cancer
Star Chart/Key: March; **5**
Type/Distance: Star cluster; 600 light years
Magnitude: +3.7
A fuzzy patch to the unaided eye; a telescope reveals many of its 1000 stars.

M81 and M82   🔭 ⊁

Constellation: Ursa Major
Star Chart/Key: March; **6**
Type/Distance: Galaxies; 12 million light years
Magnitude: +6.9 (M81); +8.4 (M82)
A pair of interacting galaxies: the spiral M81 appears as an oval blur, and the starburst M82 as a streak of light.

The Plough   👁

Constellation: Ursa Major
Star Chart/Key: April; **7**
Type/Distance: Asterism; 82–123 light years
Magnitude: Stars are roughly magnitude +2

Virgo Cluster

The seven brightest stars of the Great Bear form a large saucepan shape, called 'the Plough'.

Mizar and Alcor   👁 🔭 ⊁

Constellation: Ursa Major
Star Chart/Key: April; **8**
Type/Distance: Double star; 83 & 82 light years
Magnitude: +2.3 (Mizar); +4.0 (Alcor)
The sky's classic double star, easily separated by the unaided eye: a telescope reveals Mizar itself is a close double.

Virgo Cluster   🔭 (difficult) ⊁

Constellation: Virgo
Star Chart/Key: May; **9**
Type/Distance: Galaxy cluster; 54 million light years
Magnitude: Galaxies range from magnitude +9.4 downwards
Huge cluster of 2000 galaxies, best seen through moderate to large telescopes.

SUMMER

Antares   👁 🔭 ⊁

Constellation: Scorpius
Star Chart/Key: June; **10**
Type/Distance: Red giant; 550 light years
Magnitude: +0.96
Bright red star close to the horizon. You can spot a faint green companion with a telescope.

M13   👁 🔭 ⊁

Constellation: Hercules
Star Chart/Key: June; **11**
Type/Distance: Star cluster; 23,000 light years
Magnitude: +5.8

A faint blur to the naked eye, this ancient globular cluster is a delight seen through binoculars or a telescope. It boasts nearly a million stars.

Lagoon and Trifid Nebulae

Constellation: Sagittarius
Star Chart/Key: July;
Type/Distance: Nebulae; 5000 light years
Magnitude: +6.0 (Lagoon); +7.0 (Trifid)
While the Lagoon Nebula is just visible to the unaided eye, you'll need binoculars or a telescope to spot the Trifid. The two are in the same binocular field of view, and present a stunning photo opportunity.

Albireo

Constellation: Cygnus
Star Chart/Key: August;
Type/Distance: Double star; 430 light years
Magnitude: +3.2 (Albireo A) ; +5.1 (Albireo B)
Good binoculars reveal Albireo as being double. But you'll need a small telescope to appreciate its full glory. The brighter star appears golden; its companion shines piercing sapphire. It is the most beautiful double star in the sky.

Dumbbell Nebula

Constellation: Vulpecula
Star Chart/Key: August;
Type/Distance: Planetary nebula; 1270 light years
Magnitude: +7.5
Visible through binoculars, and a lovely sight through a small/medium telescope, this is a dying star that has puffed off its atmosphere into space.

Dumbbell Nebula

AUTUMN

Delta Cephei

Constellation: Cepheus
Star Chart/Key: September;
Type/Distance: Variable star; 890 light years
Magnitude: +3.5 to +4.4, varying over 5 days 9 hours
The classic variable star, Delta Cephei is chief of the Cepheids – stars that allow us to measure distances in the Universe (their variability time is coupled to their intrinsic luminosity). Visible to the unaided eye, but you'll need binoculars for serious observations.

Andromeda Galaxy

Constellation: Andromeda
Star Chart/Key: October;
Type/Distance: Galaxy; 2.5 million light years
Magnitude: +3.4
The nearest major galaxy to our own, the Andromeda Galaxy is easily visible to the unaided eye in unpolluted skies. Four times the width of the Full Moon, it's a great telescopic object and photographic target.

Mira

Constellation: Cetus
Star Chart/Key: November;
Type/Distance: Variable star; 300 light years
Magnitude: +2 to +10 over 332 days, although maxima and minima may vary.
Nicknamed 'the Wonderful', this distended red giant star is alarmingly variable as it swells and shrinks. At its brightest, Mira is a naked-eye object; binoculars may catch it at minimum; but you need a telescope to monitor this star. Its behaviour is unpredictable, and it's important to keep logging it.

Double Cluster

Constellation: Perseus
Star Chart/Key: November;
Type/Distance: Star clusters; 7500 light years
Magnitude: +3.7 and +3.8
A lovely sight to the unaided eye, these stunning young star clusters are sensational through binoculars or a small telescope. They're a great photographic target.

Double Cluster

Algol

Constellation: Perseus
Star Chart/Key: November;
Type/Distance: Variable star; 90 light years
Magnitude: +2.1 to +3.4 over 2 days 21 hours
Like Mira, Algol is a variable star, but not an intrinsic one. It's an 'eclipsing binary' – its brightness falls when a fainter companion star periodically passes in front of the main star. It's easily monitored by the eye, binoculars or a telescope.

WINTER
Pleiades

Constellation: Taurus
Star Chart/Key: December; **20**
Type/Distance: Star cluster; 440 light years
Magnitude: Stars range from magnitude +2.9 downwards
To the naked eye, most people can see six stars in the cluster, but it can rise to 14 for the keen-sighted. In binoculars or a telescope, they are a must-see. Astronomers have observed 1000 stars in the Pleiades.

Orion Nebula

Constellation: Orion
Star Chart/Key: January; **1**
Type/Distance: Nebula; 1340 light years
Magnitude: +4.0
A striking sight even to the unaided eye, the Orion Nebula – a star-forming region 24 light years across – hangs just below Orion's belt. Through binoculars or a small telescope, it is staggering. A photographic must!

Betelgeuse

Constellation: Orion
Star Chart/Key: January; **2**
Type/Distance: Variable star; 720 light years
Magnitude: 0.0 to +1.6
Even with the unaided eye, you can see that Betelgeuse is slightly variable over months, as the red giant star billows in and out.

M35

Constellation: Gemini
Star Chart/Key: February; **3**
Type/Distance: Star cluster; 2800 light years
Magnitude: +5.3
Just visible to the unaided eye, this cluster of around 2000 stars is a lovely sight through a small telescope.

Sirius

Constellation: Canis Major
Star Chart/Key: February; **4**
Type/Distance: Double star; 8.6 light years
Magnitude: –1.47
You can't miss the Dog Star. It's the brightest star in the sky! But you'll need a 150-mm reflecting telescope (preferably bigger) to pick out its +8.44 magnitude companion – a white dwarf nicknamed 'the Pup'.

Pleiades

Anyone buying a telescope for the first time may be in for a disappointment when they find that their views through the telescope look very different from the spectacular sights seen in photos. Actually finding the objects can be a challenge for a beginner and, once found, even a bright object such as the Orion Nebula, which photographs reveal as a colourful swirl of gas and dust, loses all its colour and detail when viewed through even a fairly large amateur telescope. Any light pollution just makes things worse. I wouldn't want to put anyone off buying a conventional telescope, as it can give wonderful views of many objects, but the instant excitement is often lacking.

However, there is now a solution. There is a new breed of smart telescope available, using what is being called Electronically Assisted Astronomy, or EAA. Actually the optical designs of the instruments themselves are pretty standard, but what has changed is the application of electronics and computing power. The telescopes currently available are really quite small compared with what you can buy for the same money from standard ranges, but the results are arguably better than those seen with a much larger instrument. Only a digital camera sensor inside the telescope makes the image, and there is no direct view so that the actual light from the object hits your eyeball. A modern smartphone or tablet is essential as it provides the interface and control software via an app, and a means of viewing and saving the image.

In essence all you need to do is to put the smart telescope outside on a clear night, switch it on and stand back. From your phone's GPS it knows its location, date and time and, having taken a quick snap of a patch of clear sky, it searches its database for a match to the stars it sees. This is known as 'plate solving', a somewhat archaic term as the 'plate' referred to is no longer a photographic plate but a digital image. Within a minute the instrument will have identified where it is pointing and can then find any object in its database that you choose from the phone app. After a short time an image of the object appears on your phone, dimly at first but then improving in appearance as you watch. Even galaxies and nebulae that are completely invisible through the eyepiece of a larger instrument magically start to show up. The final result is a colour image that looks just like those in the photos.

The Unistellar eVscope 2 has a tripod that brings the eyepiece to a convenient maximum of about 1.5 m high. The unit weighs 9 kg and a backpack carrier is available. The internal battery can run the instrument for up to ten hours.

SMART TELESCOPES

Images from the 114-mm aperture eVscope 2 have a fixed field of view of 34 × 47 arcminutes, which covers all but the largest deep-sky objects. This is the Running Man Nebula, NGC 1977, in Orion.

So how do they do it? If you have a conventional telescope you will need to spend a considerable time setting it up, even if it's a GoTo telescope that can find objects in the sky for you. If you want to take images of faint objects you usually need a bulky equatorial mount that has to be precisely aligned with the Earth's axis, then you link your laptop to the astro-camera that replaces the eyepiece and take numerous individual exposures, plus separate calibration images. You may need an independent autoguider to keep the mount pointing precisely at the object. Processing the images and achieving the final result take considerable extra time, usually indoors when the session is over.

Smart telescopes use simple altazimuth-type mountings, avoiding a lot of complexity and weight. Their drawback is that when tracking an object for a long sky exposure the field of view rotates during the shot, so stars soon start to describe circles around the centre of the image. Smart telescopes get around this either by using a mechanical derotation system within the tube or by taking only short individual exposures, typically a few seconds, then aligning and stacking them before they are displayed. This is why the images that you see build up in quality during the total exposure time.

The use of plate solving avoids the often tedious process of aligning the instrument in order that it knows what part of the sky it's viewing. The instrument's automatic initialisation process takes care of all that, and also ensures

that it has found the right part of the sky before it starts photographing the object you want to view.

WHAT'S AVAILABLE

There are two main players in the smart telescope market, Unistellar and Vaonis, both based in France.

Unistellar's two instruments are known as eVscopes, each being a 114-mm reflector of 450-mm focal length. The eVscope 2 is the only smart telescope to have what appears to be a conventional eyepiece, at the side of the tube, just like that of any small reflector. However, instead of being an optical eyepiece, this is in reality a high-definition viewscreen seen through a magnifying lens. You can also view the image on your phone, or indeed on up to ten devices that are within range of the instrument's Wi-Fi hotspot. It has a 7.7 megapixel camera, which may seem poor in comparison with even a cheap digital camera but is good for an astro-camera. Some manual intervention is needed during the setting-up stage, to check the focus of the telescope, although a convenient device called a Bahtinov mask makes this a fairly easy task.

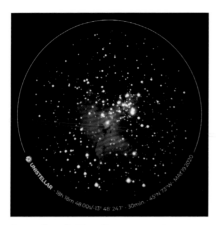

Images from the Unistellar range may be displayed with an overlay giving the object name and other details. This image shows the Lagoon Nebula, M8, in Sagittarius.

The similar but slightly cheaper eVscope eQuinox lacks the eyepiece, and has a lower resolution image chip delivering a smaller field of view, with a 4.9 megapixel camera. Both instruments are available from a range of stockists.

Lest you think that all that these telescopes are good for is to provide pretty pictures, Unistellar are teaming up with research organisations to give citizen science opportunities to record events such as transits of exoplanets in front of distant stars, producing results of scientific value.

Vaonis have gone for high-quality apochromatic refracting telescopes, with two sizes currently available and another much larger model to come. The entry-level Vespera is a 50-mm refractor of focal length 200 mm, with a 2 megapixel camera. Next up is the Stellina, an 80-mm refractor of 400 mm focal length and a 6.4 megapixel camera. Both Vaonis models have autofocus and carry a lens heater to overcome the common refractor problem of the lens, which is at the top of the instrument, dewing up.

A much larger instrument is in the pipeline – the Hyperia, a 150-mm refractor with a 61 megapixel black-and-white camera. All the other instruments have colour cameras, so this might seem a strange choice in an instrument that will cost as much as a mid-range car. But it will be equipped with a filter wheel that will permit a much wider range of imaging capabilities, including false-colour views, and is clearly aimed at a different market from the existing instruments.

Vaonis currently market their instruments by direct sale or through one specialist outlet.

ARE THEY FOR YOU?

These instruments have an immediate appeal. Many people are attracted to the idea of taking their own dramatic colour photos of the heavens, but there is a steep learning curve using conventional equipment. Smart telescopes take you right there. To use an analogy, you can derive a great deal of satisfaction from climbing a mountain. Or you can take the mountain railway to the top. Either way, the view is the same.

Cost-wise, these are very expensive instruments for their size. The prices are comparable with that of a new 125 cc motorcycle or a top-of-range large-screen TV. Yet put your new smart scope alongside a standard telescope and it looks like a space-age toy. You can achieve the same results using conventional telescopes for somewhat less money. The same image sensors used by these instruments are widely available in astro-cameras, and you can buy much larger telescopes for a fraction of the price. However, to see the same objects that you can photograph in a minute with a smart telescope you'd

The Vaonis Stellina 80-mm refracting telescope has no eyepiece so requires only a short tripod. The instrument weighs 11.2 kg.

need a much larger conventional telescope, and even then the view will lack colour and brightness.

But smart telescopes are not a complete solution. The current range lacks the resolution to give anything other than a tiny image of even the largest planet, Jupiter. To observe and photograph the planets and many other objects in detail conventional telescopes still win hands down.

There are other potential drawbacks. If you've forgotten to recharge the batteries of the telescope and your phone, you won't see a thing. The telescopes' complexity means the possibility of failures that you can't fix on the spot. The light weight of the instruments, so handy for travel, could mean spoiled images when the wind gets up.

But in terms of convenience, smart telescopes have a lot going for them. It's quite possible that in the not-too-distant future the cumbersome instruments that we are accustomed to will be regarded as

A 45-minute exposure of the Orion Nebula with the Stellina. This instrument has a wider field of view than the eVscope 2, at 60 × 47 arcminutes.

quaint and outdated. Smart telescopes also bring back the wonder of astronomy to many people for whom light pollution has meant the end of visual observing. Although they work better in dark environments, even in light-polluted suburbs these instruments will still yield views of objects that have long disappeared from sight to visual observers in those areas.

It's an often repeated saying that the best telescope is the one you use the most. And when it's crystal clear outside but biting cold, the new breed of telescope will be very popular. Just sit indoors with your phone and let the telescope do the work!

At the time of writing the only smart telescopes generally available are those from Unistellar and Vaonis, both recent start-up companies. But it's only a matter of time before the well-established manufacturers such as Sky-Watcher and Celestron bring out their own versions, perhaps at lower prices. Another innovation that we are still awaiting is an electronic eyepiece for conventional telescopes that also stacks images and displays the result on an internal screen, like the eyepiece of the eVscope 2. Electronically Assisted Astronomy is still in its infancy.

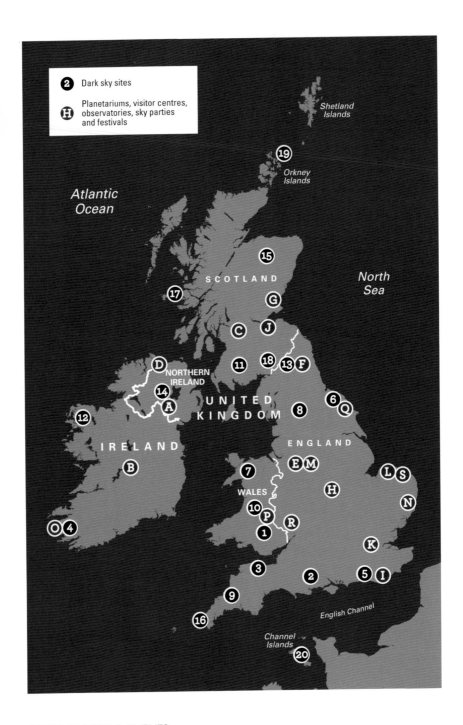

Dark sky sites

Planetariums, visitor centres, observatories, sky parties and festivals

Shetland Islands

Orkney Islands

Atlantic Ocean

North Sea

SCOTLAND

NORTHERN IRELAND

UNITED KINGDOM

IRELAND

ENGLAND

WALES

English Channel

Channel Islands

Take a break from your backyard astronomy, and head off to view the stunning skies from a protected dark-sky site. Or visit a major observatory or planetarium. Even more fun, take part in a major star party or astronomical festival.

DARK-SKY SITES

The International Dark-Sky Association, based in Tucson, Arizona, checks out the darkest places in the world. In Britain and Ireland, we have 19 places that are internationally recognised for their unsullied view of the heavens or their commitment to combating light pollution. Many are in Areas of Outstanding Natural Beauty (AONB).

DARK SKY RESERVES

Dark Sky Reserves are generally large, and consist of a very dark core region surrounded by a peripheral area where lighting is minimal. Eight out of a total of 19 worldwide are in Britain and Ireland:

1. Brecon Beacons National Park

Designated: 2013 • *Area:* 1347 sq km
Nearest towns: Brecon, Merthyr Tydfil
Website: https://www.breconbeaconspark
society.org/
Situated in the mountains of South Wales, where sheep outnumber humans 30 to 1, this Reserve is home to 33,000 people – yet lighting is controlled so that the core zone has some of the darkest skies in Wales.

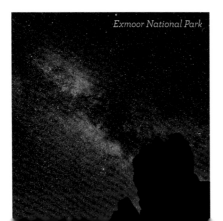

Exmoor National Park

2. Cranborne Chase

Designated: 2019 • *Area:* 981 sq km
Nearest towns: Salisbury, Shaftesbury
Website: https://cranbornechase.org.uk/
Not far from Stonehenge, Cranborne Chase is a chalk plateau rising to 277 m at Win Green. This AONB has commanding views to the west and to some extent to the north.

3. Exmoor National Park

Designated: 2011 • *Area:* 693 sq km
Nearest towns: Barnstaple, Minehead, Taunton
Website: https://www.exmoor-nationalpark.
gov.uk/enjoying/stargazing
The first Dark Sky Reserve site to be designated in these islands, Exmoor is a moorland area with much preserved history, including many monuments within the 81-sq-km core zone.

4. Kerry

Designated: 2014 • *Area:* 700 sq km
Nearest towns: Kenmare, Waterville
Website: https://www.kerrydarkskytourism.
com/
Its location between the Kerry Mountains and the Atlantic Ocean gives this Dark Sky Reserve natural protection from light pollution, yet it's readily accessible from the Wild Atlantic Way, the stunning tourist route that runs through the reserve.

5. Moore's Reserve (South Downs)

Designated: 2016 • *Area:* 1627 sq km
Nearest towns: Brighton, Portsmouth
Website: https://www.southdowns.gov.uk/
Named after the British astronomy populariser Sir Patrick Moore (1923–2012) who lived nearby, this reserve is sandwiched between London and the busy seaside resorts of Brighton and Worthing – yet it retains remarkably dark skies.

Galloway Forest Park

6. North York Moors National Park

Designated: 2020 • *Area:* 1440 sq km
Nearest towns: Scarborough, Whitby
Website: https://www.northyorkmoors.org.uk/
Despite its proximity to the busy tourist destinations of Whitby and Scarborough, the North York Moors is a largely deserted expanse of heather and bog moorland, with wide views of the night sky.

7. Snowdonia National Park

Designated: 2015 • *Area:* 2132 sq km
Nearest towns: Harlech, Porthmadog
Website: https://www.snowdonia.gov.wales/home
The national park encompasses around 10 per cent of the total land area of Wales, and the darkest skies are to be seen from the rugged central area around Mount Snowdon (1085 m).

8. Yorkshire Dales National Park

Designated: 2020 • *Area:* 2180 sq km
Nearest towns: Hawes, Kirby Lonsdale
Website: https://www.yorkshiredales.org.uk/
The largest dark-sky site in Britain and Ireland, the Yorkshire Dales National Park boasts impressive waterfalls and caves, and brilliant night skies within reach of major cities like Leeds and Manchester.

DARK SKY PARKS

Smaller regions with exceptionally low light pollution are designated Dark Sky Parks. Currently numbering eight in Britain and Ireland, more are being added every year.

9. Bodmin Moor Dark Sky Landscape

Designated: 2017 • *Area:* 208 sq km
Nearest towns: Bodmin, Launceston, Liskeard
Website: https://www.cornwall-aonb.gov.uk/bodminmoor/
This remote, rugged area of granite moorland in north-east Cornwall is a working agricultural landscape, which protects it against large-scale development that would threaten dark skies.

10. Elan Valley Estate

Designated: 2015 • *Area:* 180 sq km
Nearest towns: Aberystwyth, Rhayader
Website: https://www.elanvalley.org.uk/
The city of Birmingham purchased this Welsh valley in 1892 to construct reservoirs that would provide a regular supply of pure water. Views of the starry night over the reservoirs are particularly impressive.

11. Galloway Forest Park

Designated: 2009 • *Area:* 780 sq km
Nearest towns: Girvan, Newton Stewart
Website: https://www.forestryandland.gov.scot/visit/forest-parks/galloway-forest-park/dark-skies
Galloway Forest Park is the largest forest park in the UK, and 20 per cent has been set aside as a core area with no illumination allowed. It's a mecca not just for astronomers but for nocturnal wildlife whose lives are often disrupted elsewhere by light pollution.

12. Mayo Dark Sky Park

Designated: 2016 • *Area:* 150 sq km
Nearest towns: Ballina, Castlebar
Website: https://www.mayodarkskypark.ie/
One of the largest expanses of peat landscape in Europe, this region supports a unique diversity of bog-dwelling species. Unsuitable for agriculture, and adjoining the Atlantic Ocean, the park should enjoy pristine skies far into the future.

13. Northumberland National Park and Kielder Water & Forest Park

Designated: 2013 • *Area:* 1592 sq km
Nearest towns: Jedburgh, Rothbury

Websites: https://www.northumberlandnation alpark.org.uk/; http://www.visitkielder.com/ Near Hadrian's Wall, built to keep the Picts from Roman Britain, this Dark Sky Park was designated as a bulwark against light pollution invading the darkness of northern England. It contains the largest reservoir and most extensive forest in northern Europe.

14.   OM Dark Sky Park & Observatory

Designated: 2020 • *Area:* 15 sq km
Nearest towns: Cookstown, Magherafelt
Website: https://www.midulstercouncil.org/davaghforest
The first dark-sky place accredited in Northern Ireland, OM is set among rolling hills and is centred on the Bronze Age site of Beaghmore Stone Circles.

15.   Tomintoul and Glenlivet, Cairngorms

Designated: 2018 • *Area:* 230 sq km
Nearest towns: Dufftown, Grantown-on-Spey
Website: https://www.cairngormsdarksky-park.org/
Containing the dramatic landscape of the Cairngorm Mountains, this Dark Sky Park is home to Britain's only herd of wild reindeer. And, if the weather is cloudy, the Park also contains the Glenlivet whisky distillery!

16.   West Penwith

Designated: 2021 • *Area:* 136 sq km
Nearest towns: Penzance, St Ives
Website: https://www.cornwall-aonb.gov.uk/westpenwith

West Penwith

The very western tip of Cornwall, stretching down to Land's End, West Penwith is a wild landscape, with stunning sea views and ancient archaeological remains – some thought to be astronomically aligned.

DARK SKY COMMUNITIES

A town, village or complete island that's actively fighting light pollution can be designated a Dark Sky Community, with three listed in Britain and Ireland so far, plus one in the Channel Islands.

17.   Coll

Designated: 2013 • *Area:* 77 sq km
Website: https://visitcoll.co.uk/dark_sky/
The Scottish island of Coll is home to just 200 permanent residents, plus a myriad of birds in its extensive nature reserve. The island has adopted a light-management plan to ensure its skies remain dark.

18.   Moffat

Designated: 2016 • *Area:* 147 sq km
Website: https://visitmoffat.co.uk/
A favourite haunt of Robert Burns, this former spa town is now a tourist base for southern Scotland. Moffat has strict outdoor lighting policies to reduce light pollution in its hinterland.

19.   North Ronaldsay Dark Sky Island

Designated: 2021 • *Area:* 7 sq km
Website: https://www.northronaldsay.co.uk
The northernmost island in Orkney, North Ronaldsay has only 72 residents. Many visitors come to its bird observatory, and the island's appeal now extends to astronomers with its recent Dark Sky Community designation.

20.   Sark

Designated: 2011 • *Area:* 5 sq km
Website: http://www.sark.co.uk/
A small member of the Channel Islands near the French coast, Sark was Europe's first Dark Sky Community. Its pitch-black skies are largely due to the island's ban on public lighting and motor vehicles apart from tractors.

PLANETARIUMS, VISITOR CENTRES AND OBSERVATORIES

For a great day out under the cloudless sky of a planetarium, a tour of a world-beating observatory or an evening observing the stars, here are some leading locations. Many venues combine a planetarium (▲), visitor centre (Ⅴ) and observatory (♜).

A. Armagh Observatory and Planetarium

Website: https://www.armagh.space/
Armagh has the longest-running planetarium and the second-oldest observatory in the UK. Combine a state-of-the-art digital planetarium show with a tour of the observatory's ancient instruments (book in advance for the latter).

B. Birr Castle Demesne

Website: https://birrcastle.com/
Marvel at the well-preserved remains of the Leviathan of Parsonstown, the largest telescope in the world from 1845 to 1917. The Science Centre chronicles how the Third Earl of Rosse created his great instrument, and discovered the spiral shape of galaxies.

C. Glasgow Science Centre Planetarium

Website: https://www.glasgowsciencecentre.org/discover/our-experiences/planetarium
One of Scotland's most popular visitor attractions, Glasgow Science Centre features a 15-m diameter planetarium. After viewing the night sky in comfort, you can be awed by the giant screen of the Centre's IMAX cinema.

D. Inishowen Planetarium

Website: https://inishowenmaritime.com/planetarium/
Part of the Inishowen Maritime Museum, the planetarium is picturesquely set beside Lough Foyle. As well as putting on astronomy shows, the Maritime Museum uses the planetarium dome to project immersive ocean experiences.

E. Jodrell Bank Discovery Centre

Website: https://www.jodrellbank.net/
Grab a close-up view of the Lovell Telescope, the great radio dish that tracked rockets in the early days of the space race, downloaded pictures from the Moon and now investigates the secrets of pulsars. Other displays include exhibitions, talks and interactive activities.

F. Kielder Observatory

Website: https://kielderobservatory.org/
The Kielder Observatory, sited under some of the darkest skies in England, has a variety of telescopes for visual observing and astrophotography. It hosts some 700 events per year.

G. Mills Observatory

Website: http://www.leisureandculturedundee.com/culture/mills
On a hill above Dundee, the Mills Observatory was the UK's first purpose-built public observatory, and it carries on opening its doors to the public every clear weeknight. There's also a small planetarium and a gift shop.

H. National Space Centre

Website: https://spacecentre.co.uk/
Located on the outskirts of Leicester, this visitor centre focuses on the history – and future – of the UK in space exploration, including an original British-built Blue Streak rocket. Explore the wider Universe in the 192-seat Sir Patrick Moore planetarium.

I. Observatory Science Centre

Website: https://www.the-observatory.org/
On a hillside at Herstmonceux in Sussex, the Observatory Science Centre is located within a cluster of green domes that once housed the telescopes of the Royal Greenwich Observatory. As well as fascinating exhibits, the observatory holds regular stargazing evenings.

J. Royal Observatory, Edinburgh

Website: https://visit.roe.ac.uk/
Scotland's premier observatory no longer makes professional observations: its astronomers now build and use large telescopes on

Hawaii and in Chile. But the Edinburgh site is still active, with a visitor centre, regular astronomical talks and public stargazing evenings.

K. Royal Observatory and Peter Harrison Planetarium

Websites: https://www.rmg.co.uk/royal-observatory; https://www.rmg.co.uk/whats-on/planetarium-shows
The home of British astronomy, the Royal Observatory at Greenwich is a fascinating museum of astronomy and timekeeping: stand on the Meridian Line, with a foot in each hemisphere! The planetarium hosts a variety of astronomical shows.

STAR PARTIES AND FESTIVALS

Join in an astronomical weekend under the stars around a campfire or take part in a festival with music – there's something here for everyone to enjoy at these annual events.

L. Autumn Equinox Sky Camp

Kelling Heath, Norfolk • September
Website: https://las-skycamp.org/
Claiming to be the largest star party in the UK, the Autumn Equinox Sky Camp fills three fields with astronomers, tents, trade stands and some of the top-end amateur telescopes.

M. Blue Dot

Jodrell Bank, Cheshire • July
Website: https://www.discoverthebluedot.com/
Astronomy's answer to Glastonbury, with live music, illuminated artworks, astronomy- and science-themed tents, cosmic inflated domes, family fun and talks from leading astronomers. Too busy and bright to actually observe the sky.

N. Haw Wood

Saxmundham, Suffolk • April
Website: https://www.brecklandastro.org.uk/star-parties
Astronomers literally pitch up at Haw Wood farm for a small-scale, friendly week of stargazing, organised by local astronomical societies.

O. Skellig Star Party

Ballinskelligs, County Kerry • August
Website: https://www.facebook.com/Skellig StarParty
Ireland's leading star party is held under the pristine skies of the Kerry Dark Sky Reserve. It features talks by leading astronomers as well as night-time observing.

P. Solarsphere Astronomical and Music Festival

Builth Wells, Powys • August
Website: https://solarspherewales.co.uk/
Solarsphere is a unique mix of music and astronomical talks, family events and trade stalls by day, and astronomical observing at night.

Q. Starfest

Dalby Forest, North Yorkshire • August
Website: http://www.scarborough-ryedale-as.org.uk/saras/starfest/about-starfest/
This event attracts astronomers from all over the country for a weekend of events that can include rocket-building, talks, an astronomical pub quiz and – of course! – observing the sky.

R. Stargazers' Lounge Star Party

Lucksall Caravan and Camping Park, Herefordshire • October
Website: https://stargazerslounge.com/
Stargazers' Lounge is an online forum for amateur astronomers, but they meet in real life in Herefordshire for a weekend of talks, trade stands, socialising and skywatching.

S. Winterfest

Kelling Heath, Norfolk • December
Website: https://www.winterfestastro.co.uk/
Organised by the Birmingham Astronomical Society to give its members some respite from the city's lights, Winterfest is open to all who want to brave the December weather in pursuit of the glittering winter stars.

Many of the sites on pages 91–93 also host their own star parties or weekends: check their websites. Also see https://www.darkskiesnationalparks.org.uk/ for events.

THE AUTHOR

Nigel Henbest is an award-winning British science writer, specialising in astronomy and space. After research in radio astronomy at Cambridge, he became a consultant to both the Royal Greenwich Observatory and *New Scientist* magazine, and is a Fellow of the Royal Astronomical Society.

Originally with Heather Couper, Nigel has been writing Philip's *Stargazing* since 2005. The author of 40 other books, Nigel is a regular media commentator on breaking astronomy news. He co-founded a TV production company, where he produced acclaimed programmes and international series on astronomy and space.

Nigel divides his time between Buckinghamshire and North Carolina. He is a Future Astronaut with Virgin Galactic, and asteroid 3795 is named 'Nigel' in his honour.

ACKNOWLEDGEMENTS

PHOTOGRAPHS
Front Cover: Damian Peach. **Alamy Stock Photo:** Chrispo 91; Gary Cook 92; Keith Mason 93. **Jo Bourne:** 77. **Bernie Brown:** 11. **Dr J M Dean FRAS:** 35, 59. **Nick Hart:** 85 (bottom). **Bridget Henbest:** 96. **Nigel Henbest:** 7. **Kieran MacGregor:** 29. **NASA:** Bill Ingalls 48; Bob Franke 42; JPL 18; JPL-Caltech 24; UCLA 2-3. **Gary Palmer:** 23. **Damian Peach:** 52. **Robin Scagell:** 6, 84. **Science Photo Library:** Max Alexander 41. **Peter Shah:** 83, 85 (top). **Ralph Smith:** 65. **Unistellar:** 86, 87, 88. **Vaonis:** 89 (top and bottom). **Sara Wager – www.swagastro.com:** 47, 71. **Wikimedia:** David Moug 36. **Pete Williamson FRAS:** 1, 17.

ARTWORKS
Star maps: Wil Tirion/Philip's with extra annotation by Philip's. **Planet event charts:** Nigel Henbest/ Stellarium (www.stellarium.org). **Pages 80–82:** Chris Bell. **Page 90:** Philip's